S C H O O L
V I O L E N C E

A Reference Handbook

Other Titles in ABC-CLIO's
CONTEMPORARY
WORLD ISSUES
Series

SCHOOL
VIOLENCE

A Reference Handbook

Deborah L. Kopka

CONTEMPORARY
WORLD ISSUES

ABC-CLIO

Santa Barbara, California
Denver, Colorado
Oxford, England

Library of Congress Cataloging-in-Publication Data

Kopka, Deborah L.
    School violence : a reference handbook / Deborah Kopka
        p.   cm.—(Contemporary world issues series)
    Includes bibliographical references (p.   ) and index.
    1. School violence—United States—Prevention—Handbooks, manuals, etc.   2. Crime prevention—Youth participation—United States—Handbooks, manuals, etc.   3. Educational law and legislation—United States—Handbooks, manuals, etc.
    I. Title.   II. Series.
    LB3013.3.K68   1997   371.5′8—dc21

ISBN 0-87436-861-8 (alk. paper)   97-8977
                                                               CIP

03 02 01 00 99 98 97   10 9 8 7 6 5 4 3 2 1

ABC-CLIO, Inc.
130 Cremona Drive, P.O. Box 1911
Santa Barbara, California 93116-1911

This book is printed on acid-free paper ∞.
Manufactured in the United States of America

For our children

Contents

Preface

Violence is so prevalent in our society that even if we do not experience it personally, we cannot escape it in our entertainment and in our daily news. Identified by the federal government as one of our leading public health problems, it does not stop at any school's front door.

Since the turn of the century, educators have attempted to address such social issues with educational reform. The most recent systematic educational reform movement began in 1989 when U.S. governors committed themselves to reform our national education system around a framework of six goals. The goals they initially developed, with the addition of two more, became the Goals 2000: Educate America Act of 1994. Goal 7, Safe, Disciplined, and Alcohol- and Drug-Free Schools, states that "by the year 2000, every school in the United States will be free of drugs, violence, and the unauthorized presence of firearms and alcohol and will offer a disciplined environment conducive to learning."[1, 2]

Is Goal 7 achievable? The millennium is imminent. Yet regularly we hear of the drugs, the violence, and the weapons that seem to permeate our nation's schools. It is violence in general, and school violence in particular—that is, violence committed by or against children in grades K through 12—with which this text is concerned.

Today, the National Education Goals Panel; federal agencies such as the U.S. Department of Education and the Centers for Disease Control and Prevention; lawmakers, educators, and citizens in our 50 states; and many public and private institutions, agencies, and community organizations have been working toward Goal 7. Who are these entities that are focusing considerable money and effort on school violence prevention? What approaches are they taking? How successful have they been? How is this success being measured? And lastly, are our nation's schools still havens for learning, or has violence eroded their mission of education? This text will help you draw your own conclusions about where we as a nation stand and where we're headed when it comes to this crucial issue.

Notes

1. National Education Goals Panel. *1995 National Education Goals Report Executive Summary: Improving Education Through Family–School–Community Partnerships.* Washington, DC: U.S. Department of Education, 1995, p. 3.

2. Ibid, p. 4.

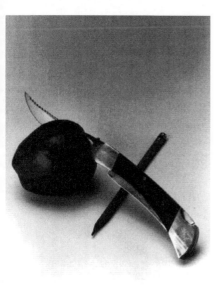

Acknowledgments

Special thanks to the following for greatly helping to guide my research efforts:

Centers for the Study and Prevention of Violence, Institute for Behavioral Science, University of Colorado at Boulder

Departments of Education in the states of Alabama, California, Colorado, Delaware, Florida, Illinois, Kansas, Kentucky, Louisiana, Maine, Minnesota, Missouri, New Hampshire, New Jersey, New Mexico, New York, Pennsylvania, South Carolina, South Dakota, Virginia, West Virginia, Wisconsin, and Wyoming

Education Development Center

Harvard School of Public Health

National Center for Injury Prevention and Control, Centers for Disease Control and Prevention

Office of Juvenile Justice and Delinquency Prevention, U.S. Department of Justice

Glenn C. Thompson, School Resource Officer, Pasadena, CA, Police Department

U.S. Department of Education

Yale University Child Study Center

Thanks also to the many organizations listed in chapter 5 that provided information and perspective on school violence prevention and control.

And thanks to Denny, as always.

Overview 1

What Is Violence?

Juvenile violence was once viewed as a social problem to be dealt with primarily by the law enforcement and judicial systems. But as violent acts become increasingly prevalent in our nation's schools, violence among youth is now recognized as a major public health problem that must be addressed by administrators, educators, family and community members, lawmakers, and health care professionals.

Since taking office in 1993, President Bill Clinton has been an ardent proponent of violence prevention, reminding us frequently that it must go hand in hand with health care. To that end, our country's lead federal agency for public health and injury control, the Centers for Disease Control and Prevention in Atlanta, is now actively involved in violence prevention efforts and the evaluation of violence prevention programs.[1]

When we think of violent acts, we tend to think only of those that produce physical harm. But many violence prevention curricula and programs extend the definition of a violent act to include verbal, visual, or physical acts intended to demean, harm, or infringe upon another's civil rights. Thus, racial epithets, white supremacy symbols, or a hard shove in a school hallway are all considered violent acts. Also, although we tend to think of school violence as that which happens only within school walls, researchers consider violence to be school related if it occurs on a school campus, on the way to or from school, or traveling to or from a school-sponsored event.

Because they are easier to quantify, the national statistics on school violence focus on incidents of physical violence, such as those involving weapons. But many incidents of perhaps less obvious types of violence—bullying a physically challenged student, for example—occur on a daily basis. The violence statistics quoted in this text represent acts of physical assault. But many of the curricula and programs discussed focus on preventing all types of physical and nonphysical violence by using conflict resolution before violence occurs.

Juvenile Violence from 1970 to the Present

During the 1960s and 1970s, when school violence was not perceived to be the national problem it is today, most school districts did not keep or report statistics on the number of juvenile arrests for acts of school violence. Nevertheless, we do have statistics from the U.S. Department of Justice on the number of juvenile arrests nationally. According to *Juvenile Offenders and Victims: A National Report* released in 1995 by the National Center for Juvenile Justice, from 1973 through 1988 the number of juvenile arrests for murder and non-negligent manslaughter, forcible rape, robbery, and aggravated assault varied with the changing size of the juvenile population. (*Juvenile Offenders and Victims* includes FBI studies, court records, and census data.)

From 1988 to 1991 there was a 38 percent jump in the rate of juvenile arrests for violent crimes. The arrest rate diminished, with juvenile arrests increasing little between 1991 and 1992. But the rapid growth from 1988 to 1992 moved the juvenile arrest rate for violent crime in the latter year well above any year since the mid-1960s (the earliest time period for which comparable statistics are available).

During the 1970s and 1980s, the proportion of juvenile violent crime cases cleared (that is, resolved) by juvenile arrest declined with the declining juvenile population, reaching its lowest level in 20 years in 1987. Unfortunately, however, the number of juvenile violent crimes began to increase between 1987 and 1992, returning to the levels of the early 1970s. Juveniles were responsible for about one in eight violent crimes in 1992, and

Figure 1 Arrests per 100,000 Juveniles Ages 10–17

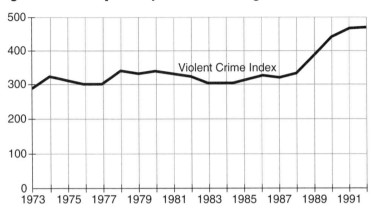

Source: FBI. *Age-Specific Arrest Rates and Race-Specific Arrest Rates for Selected Offenses, 1965–1992*, 1994. From Howard N. Snyder and Melissa Sickmund. *Juvenile Offenders and Victims: A National Report*. Washington, DC: Office of Juvenile Justice and Delinquency Prevention, 1995, p. 104.

Figure 2 Violent Crime Index Arrests per 100,000 Juveniles Ages 10–17

Source: FBI. *Age-Specific Arrest Rates and Race-Specific Arrest Rates for Selected Offenses, 1965–1992*, 1994. From Howard N. Snyder and Melissa Sickmund. *Juvenile Offenders and Victims: A National Report*. Washington, DC: Office of Juvenile Justice and Delinquency Prevention, 1995, p. 104.

accounted for more than one in six persons entering the justice system charged with a violent offense. (See Figure 1, this page.) The rapid growth in violent crime arrest rates between 1988 and 1992 is found in all racial groups.[2] (See Figure 2, this page.)

Table 3 Juvenile Arrest Projections Based on Varying Underlying Assumptions

Offense	Juvenile arrests in 1992	Projections assuming no change in arrest rates from 1992 to 2010		Projections assuming annual changes in arrest rates equal to the average increases from 1983 to 1992	
		Juvenile arrests in 2010	Increase over 1992	Juvenile arrests in 2010	Increase over 1992
Violent Crime Index	129,700	158,600	22%	261,000	101%
Murder	3,300	4,100	23	8,100	145
Forcible rape	6,300	7,700	22	10,400	66
Robbery	45,700	56,600	24	72,200	58
Aggravated assault	74,400	90,200	21	170,300	129

If juvenile arrest rates remain constant through the year 2010, the number of juvenile arrests for violent crime will increase by one-fifth; if rates increase as they have in recent history, juvenile violent crime arrests will double.

Estimates of future juvenile arrests for violent crime vary widely. Their accuracy relies on each estimate's underlying assumptions and existing data. According to *Juvenile Offenders and Victims,* two sets of estimates were developed using different assumptions. Both sets are based on age-specific arrest rates and projected population growth (controlling for racial differences).

The first set of estimates assumes that, given the projected growth in the juvenile population ages 10 to 17, the rate of juvenile violent crime arrests in 2010 will equal the rate in 1992. This means that the number of violent juvenile crime arrests would increase 22 percent between 1992 and 2010. Projected increases would be nearly equal in all offense categories. The second set of estimates assumes that juvenile violent crime arrest rates will increase annually between 1992 and 2010 in each offense category as they have in recent history (for example, from 1983 to 1992).

Assuming both population growth and continuing increases in arrest rates, the number of juvenile violent crime arrests is expected to double by 2010. The projected growth varies across crime categories. (See Table 3, this page.)[3]

Sources of Data on School Violence

Although some states require local school districts to report school violence statistics to the state legislature annually, no federal law mandates primary and secondary educational institutions to report the number of violent incidents occurring in and around schools. (Postsecondary educational institutions such as colleges and universities, on the other hand, must report and publish crime statistics.) Nevertheless, as school violence has escalated over the past several years, many agencies and organizations have solicited and maintained data related not only to school violence statistics but also to the attitudes of educators, students, and the public.

Much of the data released on school violence within the last few years comes from federal agencies, organizations, educational institutions, and assessment surveys, including:

Centers for Disease Control and Prevention (CDC)

Council of the Great City Schools

Federal Bureau of Investigation (FBI)

Gallup Organization

Harvard School of Public Health

Louis Harris and Associates, Inc.

"Metropolitan Life Survey of the American Teacher"

National Center for Health Statistics

National Education Association (NEA)

National Institute of Justice

National League of Cities

National School Boards Association

National School Safety Center (acts as a federal clearinghouse on school violence)

U.S. Department of Justice

"Youth Risk Behavior Survey" (conducted by the Youth Risk Behavior Surveillance System of the CDC, which periodically measures the prevalence of priority health-risk behaviors among youth through national, state, and local surveys)

Additional sources of data include state and local criminal justice agencies and police departments, and medical and social service agencies. It is beyond the scope of this text to chronicle exhaustively all of the data about school violence that has come from these organizations and surveys within the last 25 years. However, to get an idea of recent statistics, public opinion, and other types of information collected on this subject, it is useful to look at some of the recent, notable school crime and violence statistics issued by some of these organizations.

National Statistics

According to the federal government's first published report on school-related violent deaths, which appeared in the 12 June 1996, *Journal of the American Medical Association*, 105 people died at schools or during school-associated activities from 1992 to 1994. Eighty percent of the deaths were homicides; the rest were suicides. Seventy-six of the victims were students, 12 were school staff members, and the rest were not associated with the school. Two-thirds of the 105 deaths were traced to personal disagreements or gang activity; guns were used in 77 percent of the deaths. The deaths, which occurred in 101 schools in 25 states, were twice as common in urban schools than in suburban schools.[4]

The above statistics were the result of a three-year study conducted by researchers at the CDC who gathered school crime data from the U.S. Department of Education, the National School Safety Center, local police departments, and various information databases. The CDC has worked in violence prevention since 1983 and coordinates activities and programs in the Public Health Service to prevent youth violence.

According to 1994 statistics from the U.S. Department of Justice, almost 3 million crimes occur on or near the 85,000 school campuses in the United States each year.[5, 6] This roughly translates into about 16,000 incidents per school day.[7]

According to *Juvenile Offenders and Victims*, the U.S. Department of Justice report cited in the previous section, juveniles are most likely to commit violent acts and other crimes between 3 P.M. and 6 P.M., peaking between the end of the school day until dinnertime, when the number of incidents starts to decline. Juveniles are less likely to engage in illegal acts or to be victims of crime while in school.[8]

According to a 1993 NEA report on school safety, each day an estimated 100,000 guns are brought to school.[9]

Student Surveys

A 1995 survey conducted by Louis Harris and Associates surveyed 2,023 students in grade seven and higher in public, private, and parochial schools nationwide. This also included a nationally representative sample of students in at-risk neighborhoods characterized by a high incidence of crime, drug use, and gang activity. Released in early 1996, the survey found the following:

> 12 percent of all respondents reported carrying such weapons as bats, clubs, knives, or guns to school for protection

> 28 percent reported that they "sometimes or never" felt safe in their school buildings

> 11 percent said they had stayed home from school or cut classes because of their fear of crime or violence

> 12 percent said their fear of violence had a negative effect on their grades[10]

Interviews conducted with a representative sample of 2,508 students as part of a 1994 Harvard School of Public Health survey of students nationwide ("A Survey of Experiences, Perceptions, and Apprehensions about Guns among Young People in America") revealed the following:

> 15 percent of students at 96 public and private elementary, middle, and senior high schools said they carried a handgun

> 4 percent said they had brought a handgun to school during that year

> 9 percent said they had shot a gun at someone that year

> 11 percent said they had been shot at during the past year

> 39 percent said they knew someone personally who had been killed or injured by gunfire

59 percent said they could get a handgun if they wanted one[11]

In 1993, the *Morbidity and Mortality Weekly Report* published by the CDC reported these findings from a self-administered questionnaire given in 1992 to a representative sample of students, grades 9–12, in New York City Public Schools:

More than 31 percent reported being threatened with physical harm

Some 24 percent were involved in a physical fight at home, in school, or in the neighborhood

21 percent of the students reported carrying a weapon for one or more days during the 30 days preceding the survey

Rates for violent, potentially dangerous behaviors were substantially lower inside the school building and when going to or from school: being threatened, 14.4 percent; carrying a weapon, 12.5 percent; carrying a knife or razor, 10 percent; being involved in a physical fight, 7.7 percent; and carrying a handgun, 3.7 percent

Students who attended schools with metal detectors (18 percent) were as likely as those who attended schools without them to have carried a weapon anywhere, but were less likely to have carried a weapon inside the school building (7.8 percent versus 13.6 percent) or going to and from school (7.7 percent versus 15.2 percent)[12]

Teacher/Educator Surveys
In 1993, 720 affiliate school districts responded to a survey issued by the National School Boards Association entitled "Violence in the Schools: How America's School Boards Are Safeguarding Our Children." The survey found the following:

82 percent of schools report increasing violence over the last five years

60 percent reported weapons incidents

Three-fourths reported that their schools had dealt with violent student-on-student attacks during the past year; 13 percent reported a knifing or shooting

15 percent of schools reported the use of metal detectors

Respondents reported that they used the following methods for dealing with violence:

Suspension (78 percent)

Student conduct/discipline code (76 percent)

Collaboration with other agencies (73 percent)

School board policy (71 percent)

Alternative programs at schools (66 percent)

Staff development (62 percent)

Conflict resolution/mediation training/peer mediation (61 percent)[13]

Since 1984, Louis Harris and Associates has been conducting "The Metropolitan Life Survey of the American Teacher," which explores teachers' opinions and brings them to the attention of the U.S. public and policymakers. The 1995 survey "Old Problems, New Challenges" showed that the representative sampling of teachers considered school violence a considerable issue.

41 percent of teachers say the incidence of violence in and around schools is a serious problem

Violence was more likely to be considered serious by teachers in inner cities (72 percent) and other urban areas (54 percent), compared to those in the suburbs (41 percent), rural areas (30 percent), and small towns (28 percent)

25 percent of junior high and high school teachers say the number of students carrying handguns, knives, and other weapons to school is a serious problem, mostly in inner cities (46 percent) and other urban areas (31 percent), as compared to rural areas (24 percent), the suburbs (20 percent), and small towns (18 percent)

In 1993, one in seven teachers in urban and suburban schools had been the victim of a violent act that occurred in or around their schools[14]

National Opinion

The 1995 "Annual Gallup Poll of the Public's Attitude toward the Public Schools," which polled 1,325 adults over the age of 18 during 1994, found that fighting, violence, and gangs ranked with "lack of discipline" as the biggest problems facing schools. (In the past 26 Gallup polls, lack of discipline was cited as one of the top problems facing public schools, and as the number-one problem in 17 of the 26 polls.)

Respondents ranked the following causes of increased violence in schools as very important:

> Increased use of alcohol and drugs among school-aged youth (78 percent)
>
> Easy availability of weapons (72 percent)
>
> Growth of youth gangs (72 percent)
>
> A breakdown in the U.S. family (70 percent)
>
> Schools lacking the authority to discipline that they once had (65 percent)
>
> Increased portrayal of violence in the media (60 percent)[15]

Do Statistics Prove That the Problem Is Worsening?

A complaint echoed in teacher's lounges throughout the country at the start of every school year is, "The incoming class is the worst behaved yet." Is student behavior becoming progressively worse? Do the above statistics, many of which are drawn from representative samplings of populations, really prove that school violence has escalated into a problem of critical proportions?

According to Ron Stephens, executive director of the National School Safety Center, much of this information is indeed opinion based and thus gives cause for skepticism. Nevertheless, as indicators that the problem is worsening, he cites growth in alternative schools for disruptive students at all grade levels and recent federal and state safe school bills that ban weapon possession, increase penalties for teacher assaults, and require law enforcement agencies to share information on juvenile offenders.

Despite Stephens' assertion, some contend that the school violence problem is grossly overstated by political conservatives who want to demand charters that allow citizens to start their own schools with a public subsidy.[16]

Potential Risk Factors in Youth Violence

There are many theories about what triggers the complex human behavior called violence, and the research is ongoing. Some feel that the potential for violent behavior is inherent in the chemical makeup of the human body. Some feel that violent behavior is learned from family members, neighborhood environment, and peer groups. And some posit that violent behavior is the result of negative social forces such as poverty and lack of economic opportunity.

In reality, violence is most likely the result of a complex linkage of many risk factors. No risk factor is mutually exclusive; each has the potential to contribute to violent behavior. Physicians, scientists, researchers, educators, sociologists, and social reformers have identified some key probable risk factors in youth violence: certain physiological elements, certain socioeconomic elements, the availability of handguns, membership in a gang, drug and alcohol use, and violence in the media.

Physiological Risk Factors

Some theorize that when a child (or an adult) feels threatened by such stressors as physical abuse, noradrenaline, the "alarm hormone," stimulates body chemicals to help the child fight or flee. High levels of noradrenaline may exacerbate violent behavior.

Serotonin, the "feel-good hormone" that keeps aggression in check, has been intensively studied in human and animal research on violent behavior. It is theorized that stressors in the child's life may decrease serotonin and increase noradrenaline. This, in turn, increases the child's sensitivity to stress. Thus, the child may interpret an inadvertent behavior (an innocent gesture, for example) as an aggressive behavior and violently lash out.[17]

Children with hyperactivity, attention deficit disorder, and low intelligence are thought to be predisposed toward violence because they may lack basic problem-solving skills and the ability to tell the difference between nonviolent solutions and situations that could result in conflict. Some say that sugar and food additives cause the hyperactivity that sometimes precedes violent behavior.

Key variables to consider when looking at physiological causes of stress are each person's physiological and psychological makeup. What one child interprets as a stressor (parental fighting, for example), another child may not. What causes a violent response in one child may not even affect the behavior in another. Each child's reaction depends on how he or she processes information and is shaped by such factors and influences as injury, stress, and hormonal activity.

Socioeconomic Risk Factors

Although no single socioeconomic factor can be held solely responsible for provoking violent behavior in children, many can enmesh children in violent situations that, in turn, can trigger violent responses. Consider these probable socioeconomic causes of violence:

Domestic violence.

Poverty, which often results in depression, anxiety, and rage.

Substance abuse, which often results in child neglect.

Children born out of wedlock to homes where there is no authority figure or role model to teach them socially acceptable behavior. About one-third of all babies in the United States are born to unwed mothers. Seventy percent of juvenile court cases involve children from single-parent families.[18]

Broken homes and two-income families, which leave an estimated one in five children home alone and sometimes neglected after school.[19]

Lack of parental involvement, which is cited by more than 50 percent of all school executives as a more important factor in school violence than social class, racial or ethnic tension, gangs, alcohol and drugs, or student transiency.[20]

Peer pressure.

The presence of such outsiders at school as dropouts and unemployed neighbors who, according to one-third of school leaders, are some of the most likely instigators of school violence. High school and urban administrators seem to be most affected by unwanted visitors.[21]

The Availability of Handguns

According to findings revealed in 1994 through interviews conducted as part of the Harvard School of Public Health's "Survey of Experiences, Perceptions, and Apprehensions about

Guns among Young People in America," more than one in three young people in this country today have concluded that their chances of living to a ripe old age are likely to be cut short by gun violence.[22]

Indeed, many believe that the easy access to handguns ignites youth violence both in and out of school. According to the Children's Defense Fund, some 50,000 children in the United States were killed by guns between 1979 and 1991.[23]

Although many parents and guardians claim to keep guns and ammunition separate, children who are home alone have the access and lack of supervision that can lead to deadly consequences. Thus, many in the public health community assert that the most effective violence prevention effort would be to ban the possession, manufacture, and sale of handguns.[24]

Membership in a Gang

Today, gangs exist not only in larger urban districts but also in small suburban districts in both public and private schools. According to a 1994 report, administrators of schools with enrollments of more than 25,000 students and principals of urban schools report significant increases in gang-related incidents. Even one in four elementary principals cite an increase in gang-related incidents.[25]

A discussion of the theories and research on the psychology underlying gang culture is not within the scope of this text. Nevertheless, it must be said that gangs are strong peer groups in which violence is modeled, encouraged, and rewarded. Gang membership provides a sense of identity and belonging and thus can boost self-esteem.

Violence among gang members often demonstrates qualities valued by the gang or reinforces group solidarity by disciplining individual members. Violence among gangs often occurs over issues of status, reputation, and turf.[26]

Drug and Alcohol Use and Abuse

The use and abuse of drugs and alcohol have long been associated with violence, but no clear cause-and-effect relationship has yet been shown. In 1994, fewer than one in five administrators cited an increase in drug-related incidents in their schools. (This might indicate the positive impact of some antidrug programs.) About one-third of administrators report an increase in alcohol-related incidents of school violence. Although more than one in four elementary school principals note a rise in alcohol-related incidents, most elementary school principals report that alcohol-related incidents of violence have not been a factor in their buildings.[27]

Many cite the availability of crack cocaine, which became readily available in the mid-1980s, as a key probable cause of youth violence both in and out of school. With the advent of crack, drug dealing became a well-paid and violent business for many juveniles.[28]

Violence in the Media

According to 1993 estimates from the American Psychological Association, children watch an average of 8,000 murders and 100,000 other violent acts on television before finishing elementary school.[29] Some estimate that Saturday morning cartoons alone average 25 episodes of violence per hour.[30] How entertainment affects our behavior is the subject of so much debate and research that a comprehensive overview of the myriad issues related to this subject is outside the scope of this text. While it is true that children daily see violent acts in films, rock videos, television programs, and the nightly news, the question still remains as to what extent such violent images trigger violent behavior.

What we don't know about the media's effects on us probably equals what we do know. Some psychologists contend that children imitate the violence they see in the media. Others contend that the frequency of violence in the media overstates the amount of violence that occurs in real life and thus leads children to believe that violence is the way to solve problems. Some contend that how a child is affected by media violence depends on whether the child sees violence as rewarded or punished. Whatever argument seems the most convincing, it is still true that a child's physiological and psychological makeup will determine his or her response. A child who is not prone to aggression may not be affected by violent visual images; a child prone to aggression might be.[31]

In July 1996, Congress passed the controversial Telecommunications Bill, enthusiastically endorsed by President Bill Clinton, which calls for the installation of the antiviolence V-chip in new television sets starting in 1998. The bill also requires broadcast networks to rate their programs for violent content. Parents/guardians can then program the chip and block out programs they do not wish their children to see.

Not surprisingly, there was considerable backlash from entertainment industry leaders who claimed that the measure amounts to censorship. Channel-blocking devices can already be bought, they asserted. Also, they raised two key questions: (1) Who will set the standards for rating the violent content? The federal government? The entertainment industry? Public consensus? and (2) When do those standards, once set, become censorship?

Is the V-chip boon or boondoggle? Only time will tell. It will be 10 to 15 years before all televisions in all households have it. The television program rating system, on the other hand, began implementation in January 1997. The ratings—TV-Y (suitable for all children), TV-Y7 (for children ages 7 and above), TV-G (for all audiences), TV-PG (parental guidance suggested), TV-14 (not suitable for children under 14), and TV-M (for mature audiences only)—appear in the corner of the television screen for 15 seconds at the beginning of every program. Each network is responsible for rating its own material. News, sports programming, promos, and commercials are not rated. MTV will not rate each video, only whole program blocks.

Some complain that this system is not helpful since the networks have lumped many programs with varying degrees of violent and sexual content into the TV-PG rating so they do not lose advertisers. Many parents have voiced their preference for program ratings that describe the violence, adult language, and sexual content in each program so they can use their own discretion in determining the level of appropriateness for their children. The current rating system, however, will remain in place for a trial period of ten months after which the Federal Communications Commission can accept or reject it.[32]

There are so many variables when considering the behavioral effects of media violence that we may never fully understand just how violent images trigger violent behavior, if indeed they do. For now, a solution seems to lie in not only reducing the number of violent images children see in the media but also in early and constant reinforcement by parents/guardians, teachers, and other role models that violence is not a solution to solving real-life problems.

Despite the Risk Factors

Despite the risk factors cited above, some studies find that many adolescents exposed to them do not become delinquent. According to the Congressional Office of Technology Assessment,

"studies have found that a positive temperament, including positive mood and a tendency to evoke positive responses in others, a
high IQ, positive school and work experiences, high self-esteem,
some degree of structure in the environment, and one good relationship with a parent or other adult reduce the risk factors associated with offending."[33]

Federal Legislation Targeting School Violence

The national concern for school safety and school security
led Congress to pass two key pieces of school violence prevention legislation in 1994: the Gun-Free Schools Act and the Safe
and Drug-Free Schools and Communities Act.

Under the Gun-Free Schools Act (GFSA), every state receiving federal aid for elementary and secondary education must
require school districts to expel from school for at least one year
any student who brings a gun to school. Private schools are subject to the provisions of the GFSA. Nevertheless, private school
students who participate in programs or activities that receive
federal education dollars are subject to the one-year expulsion
requirement.[34]

The Safe and Drug-Free Schools and Communities Act
(SDFSCA) funds violence prevention and education programs
for students and training and technical assistance for teachers. It
also allocates funds to develop violence and drug prevention
programs that involve parents and coordination with the community. Fiscal year 1997 appropriations for this program were
$558,978, with fiscal year 1998 funds proposed at $620,000.[35, 36]

The GFSA and the SDFSCA have served as precursors to
many state laws related to weapons possession, alcohol, and
other drugs. Brief descriptions of some of the key state laws
related to school violence prevention, as well as further information on the GFSA and the SDFSCA, may be found in chapter 4.

Related Federal Legislation

Also signed into law in 1994, the Violent Crime Control and
Law Enforcement Act put more police officers on the streets,
funded new prison construction, imposed stiffer penalties on
violent crime (including a mandatory term of life in prison for
offenders with three or more convictions for serious violent
felonies and drug-trafficking charges), and banned deadly
assault weapons.

The act also expanded federal assistance for community-based crime prevention efforts, including programs and activities that help improve opportunities for youth, especially youth in poor and high-crime areas. More information on such federal programs can be found in *Preventing Crime & Promoting Responsibility: 50 Programs That Help Communities Help Their Youth*. (See the section in this chapter entitled "Federal Combined Strategy Programs" on page 25.)[37]

Goals 2000: Educate America Act of 1994 provides resources to states and communities for education reforms that will help students reach academic and occupational standards. This legislation comprises eight national education goals developed by our nation's governors. (For more information on the Violent Crime Control and Law Enforcement Act and the Goals 2000: Educate America Act, see chapter 4.)

The national education goals are extremely ambitious (some say they are decidedly unrealistic), and progress toward achieving them has been modest. Baseline figures were established as close as possible to 1990, the year the goals were adopted. These figures are then measured against the most recent measures of performance charted by the National Education Goals Panel. With respect to Goal Seven, "Safe, Disciplined, and Alcohol- and Drug-Free Schools":

> Overall student drug and alcohol use has increased from a baseline in 1990 of 24 percent to 1995 figures of 33 percent
>
> Sale of drugs at school has increased from 18 percent to 24 percent
>
> Victimization of tenth-grade students has decreased from 40 percent to 36 percent, but victimization of public school teachers has increased from 10 percent to 15 percent
>
> The number of tenth-grade students reporting that disruptions often interfere with teaching and learning remained the same in 1992 and 1994 at 17 percent, but secondary school teachers in 1991 and 1994 reported an increase in disruptions from 37 percent to 46 percent[38]

School Violence Prevention Strategies

A survey of the National School Boards Association (NSBA) membership showed a wide variety of violence prevention strategies in use in our schools today. According to the 1993 survey cited on page 8, "Violence in the Schools: How America's School Boards Are Safeguarding Our Children," the responding school districts were implementing more than 750 violence prevention programs.[39] (Chapter 4 and chapter 6 outline some of the key strategies and curricula now being used in school violence prevention.)

Violence prevention experts identify seven key characteristics of an effective school violence prevention program:

A comprehensive approach that recognizes violence as a complex problem that requires a multifaceted response

Early and long-term commitment that focuses on reaching children when they are young and sustaining the intervention through the 12th grade

Strong school leadership and clear student disciplinary policies that are consistently applied

Effective staff development in violence prevention strategies and incorporation of those strategies into school activities

Parental involvement with training in violence prevention, making home visits, and using parents as volunteers

Interagency partnerships and community linkages

Culturally sensitive and developmentally appropriate material[40]

Deborah Prothrow-Stith, assistant dean for Government and Community Programs at the Harvard School of Public Health and guiding force behind the highly respected Violence Prevention Curriculum for Adolescents (see page 144 of chapter 6), asserts that the following elements are essential in an ideal, systemwide school violence prevention program:

Teaching social skills (including a companion course for parents)

A peer-mentoring program

Conflict-resolution programs

After-school activities

Parenting courses (for adults and teens)

Early-intervention programs for Head Start children and victims and witnesses of violence

Dating-violence intervention programs

Extended school hours to offer a community safe haven

Gang prevention and drug prevention programs

Mentoring and job-training programs

Peer leadership and peer mediation programs[41]

Most school districts do not yet have the facilities and the human and monetary resources to fund and operate an extensive, systemwide violence prevention program. Instead, many districts are now combining educational strategies such as curricula and programs that address specific subjects or focus on certain behaviors; regulatory strategies such as laws, policing, and expulsion; and environmental and technological strategies such as metal detectors and dress codes. They are choosing their strategies based on the needs of their student population, the level of violence in their communities, and their available resources.

Educational Strategies

Most educational violence prevention strategies are curricula that assume that violence is a learned behavior. Thus, they help teach students behavior management skills, conflict resolution skills, and life skills. The Education Development Center, one of the key organizations in the field of youth violence prevention, lists 14 types of violence prevention curricula being used successfully in our nation's schools.

1. **Afrocentric curricula** aim to prevent violence through an awareness of African and African-American roots. They are designed to instill a sense of cultural identity and pride.
2. **Aggression reduction/anger management curricula** convey the message that anger is a normal human emotion. They explore healthy and unhealthy ways to express and channel anger.
3. **Conflict resolution curricula** help develop empathy; impulse control; and skills in communication, problem solving, and anger management.

4. **Crime prevention/law-related education curricula** teach students how to reduce their chances of becoming victims of crime and encourage them to develop school and community projects to reduce crime.
5. **Gang prevention/reduction curricula** build awareness of the consequences of gang membership among youth who are not yet gang members.
6. **Handgun violence prevention curricula** alert students to the risk posed by handguns and help them recognize and avoid potentially dangerous situations.
7. **Life skills training curricula** teach a range of social skills that students need for healthy development, such as problem-solving skills, decision-making skills, and strategies for resisting peer pressure or media influences.
8. **Peace education curricula** look at violence prevention interpersonally and within and among societies as a whole.
9. **Peer mediation programs** involve about 15 to 20 hours of training for students and teachers. Afterward, students identify and mediate conflicts that occur in the school.
10. **Prejudice reduction/cultural awareness curricula** attempt to overcome stereotypes and prejudices that foster violence.
11. **Promoting cooperation** is an education approach that emphasizes cooperative learning in which students achieve academic success through dependence on and accountability to each other.
12. **Role model curricula** help students learn lessons in nonviolent behavior by exploring the lives of exceptional historical or contemporary figures.
13. **Self-esteem development curricula** aim to raise students' self-esteem with the underlying assumption that doing so can raise academic performance and reduce violence.
14. **Teen dating violence/family violence/sexual assault curricula** address the increased incidents of domestic violence in recent years.[42]

Chapter 6 lists many of the key school violence prevention curricula used nationally today.

In addition to the above, one educational strategy—character education—is worth exploring in further depth. Character education attempts to teach and help students clarify their values, and to help them become more caring individuals. It is taught with enthusiasm in some states and disparaged in others. Whether praised or denounced, it produces strong reactions in educators, parents, and lawmakers alike. President Bill Clinton falls into the group that praises it. In 1995, he told the Second White House Conference on Character Building for a Democratic, Civil Society that he longs for the day when every school district in the nation has character education as "a regular part of the curriculum."[43]

Clinton asserts that it is profoundly important for young people to be taught "that it's important to tell the truth, that it's important to be trustworthy and for people to be able to rely on you, that it's important not to abuse the freedom you have by undermining other people's ability to exercise their freedom."[44] In his State of the Union address in February 1997, Clinton once again exhorted all schools to teach character education as a long-term solution to violence prevention.

Nevertheless, character education has not gained widespread national acceptance. It has strong detractors at both ends of the religious and political spectrums. Some religious liberals, for example, think it will reintroduce Christianity into the classroom. Some religious conservatives claim that it will allow teachers to impose their own religious views on students or endorse alternative lifestyles. Some people simply believe that public educators cannot and should not be trusted with teaching children about moral issues that are, in their opinion, best taught in the home.

Well aware of all viewpoints, character education curriculum developers have created materials that allow for investigation of all sides of a situation. Students are encouraged to interview their family members about controversial issues. In fact, leaders of the character education movement highly promote school-home partnerships, asserting that parents are their children's primary moral educators.

Some character education programs are integrated into existing curricula (often in English and social studies). Many have been implemented in elementary schools. But districts are now developing materials for middle school and high school students who must make increasingly complex ethical choices.

One of the key questions about character education is what values should be taught. Some state departments of education, such as New Jersey's, and local school districts, such as St. Louis, Seattle, and Chicago, have developed lists of core values. But there is no nationally agreed-upon list and no nationally adopted character education curriculum. The Aspen Declaration, an outcome of a 1992 character education conference, lists respect, responsibility, trustworthiness, caring, justice and fairness, and civic virtue and citizenship as key values thought to transcend cultural, religious, and socioeconomic boundaries.

Does teaching values prevent school violence? It may, depending on the student and the situation. A student may respond well to character education training, but the gains may be negated if he or she moves on to another teacher who does not reinforce the values. For character education to be ultimately effective, students must consistently see that unethical actions have consequences.

It is likely that character education will remain controversial. Nevertheless, well-developed character education programs delivered by well-trained, objective teachers may provide values clarification that students might not get at home, or positively reinforce the moral training they do receive from parents/ guardians and other role models.[45, 46, 47]

Regulatory Strategies

Regulatory violence prevention strategies impose academic, civil, and criminal penalties on certain unwanted behaviors to lower the risk of violence. They help establish school discipline policies and procedures that pertain to student behavior, creating alternative schools, and developing cooperative relationships with police and other government agencies. Such strategies include:

Community policing

Youth curfews

School policing

Weapon-carrying laws

Laws regulating sales, distribution, nature, possession, and use of firearms

Sending trained dogs into schools to find drugs

Suspensions and expulsions

The success of any regulatory strategy depends on support from the population it serves and the level of enforcement.[48] Chapter 4 details the many regulatory approaches now being used in schools nationally.

Environmental and Technological Strategies

Environmental and technological violence prevention strategies minimize hazards and risks in the environment by reducing exposure to violence and mitigating the results of it. For example, parking lots or places of frequent conflict might be monitored by surveillance cameras. The number of potential entrances to a school may be minimized. Other common environmental and technological strategies include:

Metal detectors (about one-fourth of large urban school districts in the United States use metal detectors to help reduce the number of weapons in schools)

Increased lighting

Identification cards

Surveillance cameras

Dress codes, uniforms, or restrictions on clothing (i.e., no gang colors, hats, jackets, or insignias—even shoelaces must be black)

Drive-by shooting drills in addition to fire drills

Random locker checks

Transparent book bags

Closed-circuit television cameras on school buses

Ultimately, it is impossible to secure a school completely. Large buildings have as many as 50 exits that, due to fire code, must remain unlocked to allow for quick escape. Despite tougher security and a new closed-campus lunch policy, for example, violent incidents rose 20 percent in 1992 in District of Columbia schools.[49]

School Uniforms

President Bill Clinton is actively encouraging the adoption of uniforms in the public schools. In 1996 he asked the U.S. Department of Education to distribute to our nation's 15,000 school districts a *Manual on School Uniforms* that offers guidelines for formulating and implementing a uniform policy and details potential benefits such as decreased violence, theft, and gang activity, and increased discipline and concentration on schoolwork. Although some teachers report positive effects—

students are better behaved and focused when wearing uniforms, for example—to date there is no methodological research to prove that wearing uniforms has an effect at all.

Proponents of a mandatory uniform policy say that wearing of uniforms returns order to the classroom and thus fosters a better learning environment. Opponents say such a policy imposes an unfair penalty on students who should learn to make choices based on their own values instead of on arbitrary rules. Opponents also claim that uniforms impair students' freedom of expression.

In 1994, the Long Beach Unified School District in California enacted the nation's first mandatory school uniform dress code (California Senate Bill 1269) for all of its elementary and middle school students, beginning with the 1994–1995 school year. District officials claim that all categories of school crime have plummeted and that student attendance was at its highest rate in the history of Long Beach schools at the completion of the 1995–1996 school year. The district now plans to expand its mandatory uniform policy to its high school students and says that some 16 states have adopted school dress code legislation based on Senate Bill 1269.

Educators seem to favor the idea of school uniforms. Some 70 percent of the 5,500 middle school and secondary school principals surveyed at the National Association of Secondary School Principals Annual Conference in 1996 indicated that requiring students to wear uniforms would reduce violent incidents and discipline problems.[50, 51]

Alternative Settings

Alternative settings, either separate rooms or separate schools, are an additional environmental violence prevention strategy. They are designed to remove dangerous and/or chronically disruptive students from the classroom and meet their educational needs in an alternative environment. Alternative schools typically have a small number of students; provide self-paced instruction, peer counseling, and leadership training; and encourage the involvement of students' parents or guardians.

Some alternative settings are reporting success. One study of 18 alternative high schools found that student behavior was rarely a problem. However, when close control was introduced into one alternative program, delinquent behavior increased. This leads to the conclusion that even in an alternative setting, program structure appears to influence behavior.[52]

The Yale University School Development Program

One highly respected environmental strategy is the Yale University School Development Program spearheaded by Dr. James Comer at the Yale University Child Study Center. For more than a quarter-century, the School Development Program has brought together teachers, administrators, students, and parents to develop a comprehensive plan of social and academic goals to help positively change the overall environment of a school.

The program now operates in more than 600 schools. Although it originally addressed the needs of urban students and schools, it is now being implemented in many diverse communities. It also provides information and assistance to help schools of education, state education departments, and other agencies make their policies and practices more child-centered. (For more information on the Yale University School Development Program, see chapter 6.)

Federal Combined Strategy Programs

There are many federal programs offering communities the expertise, technical assistance, and financial resources to develop and implement local programs in youth violence prevention. The programs combine several strategies, such as classroom instruction, family involvement, vocational activities, after-school activities, job placement, and support services, and are provided in such places as service facilities, homes, schools, community centers, and treatment centers. They address all youth, not just youth at risk or youth already in the juvenile justice system. They also emphasize the importance of involving children, families, and neighborhoods.

Some notable federal programs that combine youth violence prevention strategies are:

The Drug Abuse Resistance Education program (DARE), which helps youth make healthy decisions about peer pressure, violence prevention, and drug abuse

Even Start, a family-focused program that helps improve educational opportunities for low-income families through the integration of early childhood education, adult literacy, and parental education into a family literacy program

Gang Resistance Education and Training (GREAT), which helps children resist the pressure to join gangs and to resolve conflicts without resorting to violence

Job Corps, which provides education, training, and employment for disadvantaged youth.[53]

Preventing Crime & Promoting Responsibility: 50 Programs That Help Communities Help Their Youth, published by the President's Crime Prevention Council one year after passage of the Violent Crime Control and Law Enforcement Act of 1994, gives a comprehensive overview of key federal combined strategy programs. This catalog is designed to help communities explore and implement youth crime and violence prevention efforts tailored to local resources. In addition to federal programs, many communities throughout the country provide such strategies as recreational after-school programs, foster care programs for abused youth, crisis management services to deal with violent events, programs for academic enhancement, midnight sports leagues, dropout prevention, and employment training.

Evaluations of School Violence Prevention Efforts

Creating and implementing impact evaluations depend on obtaining grants or private funds, and on skilled research and evaluation staff. To date, most school violence prevention interventions have not been rigorously evaluated, primarily due to lack of funding and trained personnel.

To be meaningful, the evaluations must be rigorous studies that use scientific research methods to estimate to what extent certain outcomes occur (for example, reductions in the prevalence of violence) because of program participation. Design issues include collection of data on impact (such as fewer fights) and outcome measures (such as reduced injuries). To determine whether violence prevention programs really cause behavioral change, evaluators should compare the outcomes achieved by students in randomly assigned treatment and control groups.[54]

In a paper entitled "What Works in Reducing Adolescent Violence: An Empirical Review of the Field," Patrick Tolan, associate professor of psychiatry and psychology at the University of Illinois at Chicago, and Nancy Guerra, also of the University of Illinois, assert that "it is not uncommon to find groups claiming the effectiveness of a [violence prevention] program simply because it serves a large number of persons or has existed for a substantial period of time, or because testimonials have been collected from clients and authority figures. Although these may represent desirable features of interventions, they have been too often persuasive in place of any demonstrated effects."[55]

Does the lack of evaluation mean that violence prevention interventions are ineffective? No, says the Children's Safety Network, Adolescent Violence Prevention Resource Center at the Education Development Center. It simply means that violence prevention is a young field. (Violence was only defined as a public health problem in the mid-1980s.)

According to the Children's Safety Network, there are elements of school violence prevention programs that appear to increase their effectiveness:

Beginning in early grades before violent behavior begins

Conflict resolution to help children recognize a violent conflict, understand how it escalates, and learn how to de-escalate it

Mediation skills that empower students to help each other resolve conflicts without adult involvement

Developing skills in critical thinking, problem solving, communication, impulse control, empathy, and resistance to peer pressure

Family involvement

A teacher-training component

Lessons that teach students how to use these skills

Developmental and cultural appropriateness that appeals to varied learning styles[56]

One key program reporting success is the Positive Adolescent Choices Training (PACT) developed by researchers at Wright State University in Dayton, Ohio. This educational violence prevention approach trains African-American and other high-risk youth in pro-social and anger management skills. PACT is one of the few violence prevention programs in the United States that has tracked long-term behavioral outcomes for its trainees and for a control group of untrained youth with similar characteristics.

For the 1992 school year, PACT program participants had a 50 percent reduction in incidents of physical aggression; the control group had a 25 percent increase. Second-semester PACT participants had a 53 percent reduction, while the control group had a 56 percent increase.[57] (For more information on PACT, see the section entitled "Notable Violence Prevention Curricula and Programs" in chapter 6.)

The Resolving Conflict Creatively Program (RCCP) promotes effective instruction in creative conflict resolution and intergroup relations for students in grades pre-K through 12. In a 1988–1989 evaluation of RCCP, 66 percent of the teachers surveyed said they observed less student name-calling and fewer verbal put-downs, 89 percent agreed that the mediation program helped students take more responsibility for solving their own problems, and 71 percent reported that students demonstrated less physical violence.[58] (For more information on the RCCP, see the section entitled "Notable Violence Prevention Curricula and Programs" in chapter 6.)

The federal government is sponsoring the largest evaluation project thus far. Three federal agencies—the CDC, the National Institute of Justice, and the National Institute for Mental Health—awarded about 26 grants totaling approximately $28 million to study the effectiveness of school-based violence interventions during fiscal years 1993 and 1994. The results should be available before 2000 and will help determine which programs work best at violence prevention.[59] Twelve of the programs being evaluated are targeted strategies, all but two are school-based programs, and three are community demonstration projects. The RCCP program is among those being evaluated.[60]

The Safe and Drug-Free Schools and Communities Act of 1994 authorized up to $1 million for a national impact evaluation. To encourage community-wide strategies, local education agencies must develop their drug and violence prevention plans in cooperation with local government, businesses, parents, medical and law enforcement professionals, and community-based organizations.[61] The act also authorized up to $25 million in discretionary funding for evaluation of national programs.[62]

Not everyone puts faith in impact evaluations or statistics. To say that a curriculum has not been sufficiently evaluated "because it hasn't been replicated in 10 different places—I don't buy that," says Gwendolyn Cooke, the director of urban services at the National Association of Secondary School Principals and a former middle school principal in Baltimore. "If it makes a difference in my school, and I have a reduction of 10 percent in some problem, those materials are O.K. by me, and I don't need researchers" to say it works.[63]

Where the Solution Lies

According to twentieth-century philosopher/educator John Dewey, schools reflect the values and problems inherent in society. If it is true that the violence in society and schools are linked, then all of us—violence prevention experts, educators, family members, health care workers, students, lawmakers, community activists, and local citizens—must work together to make National Education Goal 7 a reality. Below are 15 solutions offered by researchers, educators, and violence prevention experts that will help prevent violent behavior both inside and outside of school.

1. Teach children conflict resolution skills as early as possible
2. Ban handguns
3. Promote responsibility in the media to produce nonviolent television programs, films, and rock videos
4. Promote responsible children's television programming that addresses such issues as conflict resolution
5. Invest money and programs in communities at risk for violence
6. Start a national day-care program that includes parent education
7. Allow schools to serve as neighborhood centers for evening classes in parenting, family living skills, job training, and adult education, in collaboration with social agencies and service organizations
8. Create more jobs and vocational programs for youth
9. Coordinate communication among youth, parents, schools, police, and communities
10. Keep schools small so teachers can devote more time to each student
11. Permanently separate the habitual, violent offenders from the general school population
12. Establish violence prevention as a long-term priority in school districts
13. Include violence prevention as part of school-based health services

    14. Evaluate programs and other interventions imple-
mented in each school

    15. Volunteer time in the schools and in the communities,
acting as a supportive, positive role model for children

Researchers generally agree that any program must be tailored to each school and student population. According to Renee
Wilson-Brewer, former director of the National Network of
Violence Prevention Practitioners at the Education Development
Center, "If you're going to do violence prevention the right way,
it would make sense to really understand the school system—
the student population, the faculty population...the kinds of
violence that have occurred, the community, and its social organization and lack of organization." It is a time-consuming and
difficult task, she admits. "But unless you do that, you're not
really able to create a program that really responds to the need of
the population you're hoping to affect."[64]

We don't yet have, and we may never have, definitive
answers as to "what works" in preventing school violence.
Whatever violence prevention programs and strategies schools
adopt, we must remember that teachers are not educated and
licensed to solve all of society's ills in the classroom.

While the search for solutions continues, each of us can
work within our homes, our schools, and our communities to
provide the role modeling, the relationships, and the guidance
that children need for a healthy present and a hope-filled future.
In the long run, the gifts of time and attention that each of us
gives our nation's children may be the most effective violence
prevention strategies of all.

Notes

1. Jeffrey H. Coben, et al. "A Primer on School Violence Prevention."
Journal of School Health 64: 8 (October 1994): 309.

2. Howard N. Snyder and Melissa Sickmund. *Juvenile Offenders and
Victims: A National Report.* Washington, DC: Office of Juvenile Justice
and Delinquency Prevention, 1995, pp. 104, 105.

3. Ibid., p. 111.

4. Jessica Portner. "Study Tracks Violent Deaths at School or Related
Activities." *Education Week* (June 19, 1996).

5. Jeffrey H. Coben, et al. "A Primer on School Violence Prevention."

6. Thomas Toch and Marc Silver. "Violence in Schools." *U.S. News &
World Report* 116: 18 (November 8, 1993): 30.

7. Dorothy Cheek. "America's Schools Experience Escalating Violence among Students." *Nation's Cities Weekly* 17: 6 (February 7, 1994): 13.

8. Howard N. Snyder and Melissa Sickmund. *Juvenile Offenders and Victims: A National Report*, p. 30.

9. Jon D. Hull. "The Knife in the Book Bag." *Time* 141: 6 (February 8, 1993): 37.

10. Jessica Portner. "Poll Finds Fear of Crime Alters Student Routines." *Education Week* (January 17, 1996): 5.

11. Dorothy Cheek. "America's Schools Experience Escalating Violence among Students."

12. National School Safety Center. "Notable School Crime and Violence Statistics" (compilation of published statistics), May 1995.

13. Ibid.

14. Louis Harris and Associates, Inc. *The Metropolitan Life Survey of the American Teacher 1984–1995: Old Problems, New Challenges*. New York: Louis Harris and Associates, Inc., 1995, p. 25.

15. National School Safety Center. "Notable School Crime and Violence Statistics."

16. Ann Dykman. "Hardship Duty: A Rising Tide of Youth Violence Has Teachers Worried about the Safety of Their Workplace." *Techniques* 71: 6 (September 1996): 18.

17. Sandra Arbetter. "Violence—A Growing Threat." *Current Health* 21: 6 (February 1995): 6, 7.

18. Thomas Toch and Marc Silver. "Violence in Schools."

19. Ibid.

20. James E. Boothe, et al. "America's Schools Confront Violence." *USA Today* (Magazine) 122: 2584 (January 1994): 33.

21. Ibid.

22. Dorothy Cheek. "America's Schools Experience Escalating Violence among Students."

23. Ann Dykman. "Hardship Duty: A Rising Tide of Youth Violence Has Teachers Worried about the Safety of Their Workplace," p. 20.

24. Marc Posner. "Research Raises Troubling Questions about Violence Prevention Programs." *Harvard Education Letter* X: 3 (May/June 1994): 3.

25. James E. Boothe, et al. "America's Schools Confront Violence."

26. Albert J. Reiss, Jr., and Jeffrey A. Roth, eds. "Perspectives on Violence," in *Understanding and Preventing Violence*. Washington, DC: National Academy Press, 1993, p. 142.

27. James E. Boothe, et al. "America's Schools Confront Violence."

28. Ann Dykman. "Hardship Duty: A Rising Tide of Youth Violence Has Teachers Worried about the Safety of Their Workplace," p. 19.

29. Thomas Toch and Marc Silver. "Violence in Schools."

30. Ann Dykman. "Hardship Duty: A Rising Tide of Youth Violence Has Teachers Worried about the Safety of Their Workplace," p. 20.

31. John Leland. "Violence, Reel to Real." *Newsweek* (December 11, 1995): 46.

32. Sarah Cohen. "Trial TV Rating System Starts amid Controversy." *Electronic News* (January 6, 1997): 6.

33. Richard A Mendel. *Prevention or Pork? A Hard-Headed Look at Youth-Oriented Anti-Crime Programs.* Washington, DC: American Youth Policy Forum, 1995, p. 6.

34. U.S. Department of Education Office of Elementary and Secondary Education. Unpublished letter of August 1, 1994, to the superintendent of public instruction for the State of Idaho (with attachments) providing guidance concerning state and local responsibilities under the Gun-Free Schools Act of 1994.

35. *School Safety: Promising Initiatives for Addressing School Violence (Report to the Ranking Minority Member, Subcommittee on Children and Families, Committee on Labor and Human Resources, U.S. Senate).* Washington, DC: U.S. General Accounting Office, April 1995, p. 3.

36. "Final Fiscal 1997 Appropriations and President Clinton's Fiscal 1998 Proposals." *Education Week* (February 19, 1997): 16, 17.

37. President's Crime Prevention Council. *Preventing Crime & Promoting Responsibility: 50 Programs that Help Communities Help Their Youth.* Washington, DC: U.S. Government Printing Office, September 1995, p. 1.

38. National Education Goals Panel. *1995 National Education Goals Report Executive Summary: Improving Education through Family-School-Community Partnerships*, p. 9.

39. *School Safety: Promising Initiatives for Addressing School Violence (Report to the Ranking Minority Member, Subcommittee on Children and Families, Committee on Labor and Human Resources, U.S. Senate)*, p. 4.

40. Ibid., pp. 2, 11–13.

41. Deborah Prothrow-Stith. "Building Violence Prevention into the Curriculum." *The School Administrator* (April 1994): 11.

42. Children's Safety Network, Adolescent Violence Prevention Resource Center. *Taking Action To Prevent Adolescent Violence: Educational Resources for Schools and Community Organizations.* Newton, MA: Education Development Center, Inc., 1995, pp. viii–x.

43. Millicent Lawton. "Clinton Urges Key Place for Character Education in Curriculum." *Education Week* (May 31, 1995): 9.

44. Ibid.

45. Roger Rosenblatt. "Teaching Johnny to Be Good." *New York Times* (Magazine) (April 30, 1995): 36.

46. Stephen Bates. "A Textbook of Virtues." *Education Life* (Supplement to the *New York Times*) (January 8, 1995): 16.

47. "Guidelines from a Character-Education 'Manifesto.'" *Education Week* (May 29, 1996): 31.

48. Jeffrey H. Coben, et al. "A Primer on School Violence Prevention."

49. Thomas Toch and Marc Silver. "Violence in Schools."

50. Jessica Portner. "Department To Issue Guidelines on School Uniforms." *Education Week* (March 6, 1996): 27.

51. Kathleen L. Paliokas and Ray C. Rist. "School Uniforms: Do They Reduce Violence—Or Just Make Us Feel Better?" *Education Week* (April 3, 1996): 37.

52. Goal 6 Work Group, Office of Educational Research and Improvement. *Reaching the Goals: Goal 6: Safe, Disciplined, and Drug-Free Schools*. Washington, DC: U.S. Department of Education, September 1993, p. 11.

53. President's Crime Prevention Council. *Preventing Crime & Promoting Responsibility: 50 Programs That Help Communities Help Their Youth*, pp. 42, 44, 49, 57.

54. *School Safety: Promising Initiatives for Addressing School Violence (Report to the Ranking Minority Member, Subcommittee on Children and Families, Committee on Labor and Human Resources, U.S. Senate)*, pp. 10, 11.

55. Patrick Tolan and Nancy Guerra. *What Works in Reducing Adolescent Violence: An Empirical Review of the Field*. Boulder, CO: The Center for the Study and Prevention of Violence, Institute of Behavioral Sciences, University of Colorado, July 1994, p. 1.

56. Children's Safety Network, Adolescent Violence Prevention Resource Center. *Taking Action To Prevent Adolescent Violence: Educational Resources for Schools and Community Organizations*, p. xviii.

57. *School Safety: Promising Initiatives for Addressing School Violence (Report to the Ranking Minority Member, Subcommittee on Children and Families, Committee on Labor and Human Resources, U.S. Senate)*, pp. 28–30.

58. Ibid., pp. 32–34.

59. Ibid., p. 43.

60. Millicent Lawton. "Schools Embrace Violence-Prevention Curricula." *Education Week* 14: 10 (November 9, 1994): 1, 10–11.

61. U.S. Department of Education. "Safe and Drug-Free Schools and Communities: What's New" (unpublished material).

62. *School Safety: Promising Initiatives for Addressing School Violence (Report to the Ranking Minority Member, Subcommittee on Children and Families, Committee on Labor and Human Resources, U.S. Senate)*, p. 13.

63. Millicent Lawton. "Schools Embrace Violence-Prevention Curricula."

64. Ibid.

Chronology 2

Although some states require local school districts to report incidents of school violence, no federal law mandates primary and secondary schools to do so. As a result, statistics on juvenile arrests and convictions issued by the federal Office of Juvenile Justice and Delinquency Prevention do not specifically report incidents involving school violence. Thus, we have no chronology of national school crime statistics. We do, however, have a chronology of the youth violence prevention efforts of federal and state policymakers, health care workers, researchers, educators, and youth advocacy organizations over the last 30 years. Although it is still early to rigorously evaluate the long-term effect of most interventions and legislation, it is safe to say that they have laid a firm foundation for school violence prevention efforts both now and in the future.

1968   The Yale School Development Program began operation under the development and direction of James P. Comer, M.D., of the Yale School of Medicine.

1973–1988   During this period of time, according to the National Center for Juvenile Justice, the number of juvenile arrests for murder and non-negligent manslaughter, forcible rape, robbery, and aggravated assault varies with the changing size of the juvenile population.

1977   The National Alliance for Safe Schools is founded with the purpose of providing technical assistance, training, and research to school districts concerned with increased incidents of serious, disruptive student behavior.

1979–1991 During this period of time, according to the Children's Defense Fund, some 50,000 children in the United States are killed by guns.

1983   The Centers for Disease Control and Prevention (CDC) in Atlanta begins working in violence prevention, coordinating activities and programs in the Public Health Service to prevent youth violence.

Mid-1980s Crack cocaine becomes readily available and makes drug dealing a well-paid and violent business for many juveniles.

Violence is defined by the U.S. government as a public health problem.

1985   The "Resolving Conflict Creatively Program" begins implementation under the development and direction of current national director and cofounder Linda Lantieri.

1987   The proportion of juvenile violent crime cases resolved by juvenile arrest reaches its lowest level in 20 years.

Deborah Prothrow-Stith of the Harvard School of Public Health develops and writes the first violence prevention curriculum for schools and communities entitled "Violence Prevention Curriculum for Adolescents."

1988–1992 The rate of juvenile arrests for violent crime between 1988 and 1991 jumps to 38 percent. The juvenile arrest rate diminishes between 1991 and

1992, but the rapid growth from 1988 to 1992 moves the juvenile arrest rate for violent crime in 1992 well above any year since the mid-1960s. The growth is found in all racial groups.

1989   Positive Adolescent Choices Training (PACT) begins implementation in a middle school setting in cooperation with Dayton, Ohio, public schools.

U.S. governors meet in Charlottesville, Virginia, and commit themselves to a nationwide effort to reform education around a core set of six goals for improving the education system. These original six goals, with the addition of two more, were formalized into law in 1994 in the Goals 2000: Educate America Act.

1992   Juveniles are responsible for about one in eight violent crimes and account for more than one in six persons entering the justice system charged with a violent offense.

The Aspen Declaration, an outcome of a 1992 character education conference, lists respect, responsibility, trustworthiness, caring, justice and fairness, and civic virtue and citizenship as key values thought to transcend cultural, religious, and socioeconomic boundaries and thus appropriate for inclusion in a character education program.

The CDC funds 12 one- to three-year cooperative agreements to evaluate specific interventions that may reduce injuries and deaths related to interpersonal youth violence.

1993   William Jefferson Clinton becomes the 42nd U.S. president on 20 January. In his first term of office, he proves to be an ardent proponent of school violence prevention.

Richard Wilson Riley is unanimously confirmed as U.S. secretary of education.

According to a 1993 National Education Association report on school safety, each day an estimated 100,000 guns are brought to school.

1993
cont.

The CDC funds three five-year cooperative agreements to evaluate comprehensive violence prevention programs with multiple interventions.

The CDC publishes findings from a self-administered questionnaire given in 1992 to a representative sample of students, grades 9–12, in New York City public schools. More than 31 percent report being threatened with physical harm, 21 percent report carrying a weapon one or more days during the 30 days preceding the survey, and rates for violent and potentially dangerous behaviors are reported to be substantially lower inside the school building and when going to and from school.

The 1993 "Metropolitan Life Survey of the American Teacher" entitled "Violence in America's Public Schools" reveals that 41 percent of teachers say the incidence of violence in and around schools is a serious problem; violence was more likely to be considered serious by inner-city than urban teachers; 25 percent of junior high and high school teachers say the number of students carrying weapons is a serious problem, mostly in inner cities and other urban areas; and one in seven teachers in urban and suburban schools had been the victim of a violent act that occurred in or around their schools.

According to estimates of the American Psychological Association, children watch an average of 8,000 murders and 100,000 other violent acts on television before finishing elementary school.

According to a National School Boards Association report entitled "Violence in the Schools: How America's School Boards Are Safeguarding Our Children," responding school districts report implementing more than 750 types of violence prevention programs.

1994

The Goals 2000: Educate America Act, which is based on eight goals formulated by U.S. governors for improving the national education system, is signed into law. Goal 7 states that by 2000, every school in the United States will be free of drugs, violence, and the unauthorized presence of firearms and alcohol and will offer a disciplined environment conducive to learning. Additional goals for 2000 concern children's readiness for school, school completion, student achievement and citizenship, teacher education and professional development, achievement in mathematics and science, adult literacy and lifelong learning, and parental participation.

The Gun-Free Schools Act (GFSA) is signed into law. Under the GFSA, every state receiving federal aid for elementary and secondary education must enact a law requiring school districts to expel from school for at least one year any student who brings a gun to school.

The Safe and Drug-Free Schools and Communities Act is signed into law to fund school violence prevention programs, including those that enhance school security.

The Violent Crime Control and Law Enforcement Act is signed into law to put more police officers on the street, fund new prison construction, impose stricter penalties on violent crime, and expand federal assistance for community-based crime prevention efforts, including programs and activities that help improve opportunities for youth.

Interviews conducted with students as part of Harvard's "Survey of Experiences, Perceptions, and Apprehensions about Guns among Young People in America" reveal that 15 percent of students at 96 public and private elementary, middle, and senior high schools carry a handgun and 39 percent know someone personally who was killed or injured by gunfire.

According to the U.S. Department of Justice, almost 3 million crimes occur on or near the 85,000 school campuses in the United States each year—roughly 16,000 incidents per school day.

1994
cont.

A survey issued by the National School Board Association entitled "Violence in the Schools: How America's School Boards Are Safeguarding Our Children" finds that 82 percent of schools report increasing violence over the last five years, 60 percent report weapons incidents, and three-fourths report that their schools had dealt with violent student-on-student attacks during the past year.

Administrators of schools with enrollments of more than 25,000 students and principals of urban schools report significant increases in gang-related incidents. Even one in four elementary principals cite an increase in gang-related incidents.

Fewer than one in five school administrators cite an increase in drug-related incidents in their schools. About one-third report an increase in alcohol-related incidents of school violence. More than one in four elementary school principals note a rise in alcohol-related incidents.

The CDC, the National Institute of Justice, and the National Institute for Mental Health embark on a three-year, $28 million project to evaluate the effectiveness of school-based violence interventions during fiscal years 1993 and 1994. The Resolving Conflict Creatively Program is among those being evaluated.

The President's Crime Prevention Council is created by the 1994 Violent Crime Control and Law Enforcement Act to develop a catalog of federal prevention programs, coordinate prevention programs and planning across council departments, and assist communities and community-based organizations in their efforts to prevent crime.

The Long Beach Unified School District in California enacts the nation's first mandatory school uniform dress code for all elementary and middle school students, beginning with the 1994–1995 school year.

California Senate Bill 1269 is passed, stating that California schools have the right to enforce a dress code.

1995　　Clinton tells the Second White House Conference on Character Building for a Democratic Civil Society that he longs for the day when every school district in the nation has character education as "a regular part of the curriculum."

According to a 1995 report, the U.S. Department of Justice finds that juveniles are most likely to commit violent acts and other crimes between 3 P.M. and 6 P.M., peaking between the end of the day until dinnertime, when the number of incidents starts to decline. Juveniles are less likely to engage in illegal acts or to become victims of crime while in school.

The American Federation of Teachers begins its "Responsibility, Respect, Results: Lessons for Life" campaign, which has a strong antiviolence component and promotes higher academic and discipline standards.

According to a National Education Goals report, progress toward Goal 7 of the National Education Goals is modest. Overall student drug and alcohol use has increased from a baseline in 1990 of 24 percent to 1995 figures of 33 percent. Sale of drugs at school has increased from 18 percent to 24 percent. Victimization of tenth-grade students has decreased from 40 percent to 36 percent, but victimization of public school teachers has increased from 10 percent to 15 percent. The number of tenth-grade students reporting that disruptions often interfere with teaching and learning remained the same in 1992 and 1994 at 17 percent, but secondary school teachers in 1991 and 1994 reported an increase in disruptions from 37 percent to 46 percent.

The "Annual Gallup Poll of the Public's Attitude toward the Public Schools" finds that fighting, violence, and gangs, along with lack of discipline, are the biggest problems facing schools.

1996   In his State of the Union address, Clinton exhorts all schools to teach character education as a long-term solution to violence prevention.

According to a 1995 survey conducted by Louis Harris and Associates and released in 1996, students in grade seven and higher in public, private, and parochial schools nationwide revealed that fear of crime and violence leads many young people to miss school, earn lower grades, and carry weapons.

According to the federal government's first published report on school-related violent deaths, 105 people died at schools or during school-associated activities from 1992 to 1994. Eighty percent of the deaths were homicides; the rest were suicides. Seventy-six of the victims were students, 12 were school staff members, and the rest were not associated with the school. Two-thirds of the 105 deaths were traced to personal disagreements or gang activity; guns were used in 77 percent of the deaths. The deaths, which occurred in 101 schools in 25 states, were twice as common in urban schools than in suburban schools.

With Clinton's enthusiastic endorsement, Congress passes the controversial Telecommunications Bill, which deregulates the television industry and calls for the installation of the antiviolence V-chip in new television sets. The bill requires broadcast networks to rate their programs by January 1997 for violent content. Parents/guardians can then program the chip and block out programs coded for violent content.

The U.S. Department of Education distributes to the country's 15,000 school districts a new *Manual on School Uniforms* that offers guidelines for formulating and implementing a uniform policy.

Some 70 percent of 5,500 middle school and secondary school principals surveyed at the National Association of Secondary School Principals Annual Conference indicate that requiring students to wear uniforms would reduce violent incidents and discipline problems.

1997   The television program rating system, an outgrowth of the Telecommunications Bill of 1996, begins implementation in January on a ten-month trial basis. Some television executives claim that the ratings amount to censorship. Some parents and educators assert that the ratings are age-based and urge for content-based ratings that would better allow parents to determine appropriateness of programming for their children. Congress and the Federal Communications Commission (FCC) will hold hearings in 1997 to discuss the system. If they decide it needs improvement, the FCC will devise its own.

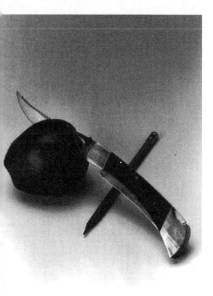

Biographical Sketches

3

Those who have made a name for themselves in school violence prevention are the educators, researchers, and health care professionals who have developed violence prevention programs, curriculums, and organizations; and the politicians and lawmakers who have championed violence prevention legislation. Nevertheless, many whose names will never be known contribute greatly to youth violence prevention efforts. Researchers at the Centers for Disease Control and Prevention study violence as intensely as they study diseases and occupational hazards. Parents, guardians, relatives, and concerned citizens serve as role models for youth both in the home and in the community. Police not only enforce regulatory strategies designed to reduce violence but also form partnerships with schools to establish student discipline policies. Media professionals create thought-provoking books, films, videos, and television programming that promote responsible action.

It is, however, our nation's teachers who perhaps play the most significant role in school violence prevention. Daily they help students manage anger, engage in school projects to reduce crime, become aware of the risks of weapons, learn healthy social skills, and examine the stereotypes and prejudices that foster violence. As a result of our teachers' constant efforts, students ultimately become more caring and understanding—qualities that help prevent conflict or resolve it before it escalates into violence. The people profiled below represent only a fraction of those working toward eliminating crime and violence in our schools.

Peter D. Blauvelt (b. 1935)

Peter D. Blauvelt is president, CEO, and cofounder of the National Alliance for Safe Schools, a nonprofit research, training, and technical assistance corporation dedicated to the promotion of safe and orderly schools. Since the inception of this organization in 1977, Blauvelt has designed and conducted hundreds of workshops for school administrators, teachers, students, and parents. He also has helped develop the School Security Assessment model that is now being used successfully in school districts across the country.

Blauvelt's background includes 24 years as director of security for the Prince George's County public schools in Maryland, three years as a special agent for the Naval Investigative Service, and seven years as a detective with the Metropolitan Police Department in Washington, D.C.

Blauvelt has a degree in General Studies, with a major and a minor in criminology, from the University of Maryland. He has written three books on school safety, the most recent of which is *Blauvelt on Making Your Schools Safe*. He has also written numerous articles for professional publications and is certified and acknowledged as an expert in the field of school security.

William Jefferson (Bill) Clinton (b. 1946)

William Jefferson (Bill) Clinton was sworn in as 42nd president of the United States on 20 January 1993. He has been an ardent proponent of school violence prevention, reminding Americans frequently that violence prevention and health care must go hand in hand. In 1994 alone, he enthusiastically supported and signed the Goals 2000: Educate America Act, the Gun-Free Schools Act, and the Safe and Drug-Free Schools and Communities Act. In 1996 he signed the Telecommunications Bill, which requires new televisions to include a V-chip that allows viewers to block programming they consider too graphic and/or violent.

Clinton received a bachelor's degree from Georgetown University in 1968 and a law degree from Yale University Law

School in 1973. From 1968 to 1970 he studied at Oxford University in England as a Rhodes Scholar.

He began his political career in 1974 with an unsuccessful campaign for Congress. Two years later, he was elected attorney general of Arkansas—a post he held for a single term before being elected governor in 1978. He lost a reelection bid in 1980, but was returned to office in 1982 and served for five terms, holding that position longer than all but one of his predecessors, until his election to the presidency in 1992.

Clinton served as chairperson of the Democratic Leadership Council in 1990–1991, the National Governors' Association in 1986–1987, the Education Commission of the States in 1986–1987, and the Lower Mississippi Delta Development Commission in 1989–1990. He has also taught at the University of Arkansas law school and has been an attorney in private practice in Little Rock.

James P. Comer (b. 1934)

James P. Comer, M.D. is currently the Maurice Falk Professor of Child Psychiatry and director of the School Development Program at the Yale Child Study Center. He is also associate dean of the Yale School of Medicine, where he is in charge of student evaluation and progress.

For more than 25 years, Comer's School Development Program, now being used in more than 600 schools in 82 school districts in 26 states, has been transforming schools into places where students learn, develop, and thrive. The mission of the School Development Program is to bring together teachers, administrators, students, and parents to develop a comprehensive plan of social and academic goals to help change the culture of a school. His work is described in his books *School Power* and *Rallying the Whole Village: The Comer Process for Reforming Education.*

His interest in the historical and contemporary economic and resultant political, economic, and social circumstances contributing to black and white racial conflict in the United States is described in his book *Beyond Black and White*. His interest in the traditional and new issues involved in child rearing as a result of scientific and technological changes in society since the 1940s was addressed in his monthly column in *Parents Magazine* between 1978 and 1993, to which he is still a contributing editor. His special interest in the rearing of African-American children is reflected in his books *Black Child Care* and *Magpie's American Dream*.

Comer has lectured, observed, and/or discussed child care, school, and/or social welfare programs and conditions in London, England; Nairobi, Kenya; Jerusalem, Israel; Stockholm, Sweden; Paris, France; Dakar, Senegal; Tokyo, Japan; Peking, Tachai, Nanking, Shanghai, Hangchow, Kweilin, and Canton in the People's Republic of China; Siena, Italy; and Marbach Castle, Germany. Consultancies include the Children's Television Workshop *(Sesame Street, Electric Company)*, the Public Committee on Mental Health chaired by Rosalynn Carter, and a preeducation summit meeting with President George Bush and Secretary of Education Lauro F. Cavazos.

Comer holds an A.B. from Indiana University, an M.D. from Howard University's College of Medicine, a Master of Public Health degree from the University of Michigan School of Public Health, and 35 honorary degrees. He did his training in psychiatry at the Yale School of Medicine, the Yale Child Study Center, and the Hillcrest Children's Center in Washington, D.C. Among his numerous awards are the Rockefeller Public Service Award, *Newsweek's* "25 Americans on the Cutting Edge," and a Special Presidential Commendation from the American Psychiatric Association.

Linda Lantieri (b. 1948)

Linda Lantieri is an internationally known peace educator, conflict resolution and intergroup relations specialist, keynote speaker, and Fulbright scholar. She is recognized as a highly effective advocate at the national level for helping to make our schools, homes, and communities caring and violence-free growing environments. She is currently national director and cofounder of the highly acclaimed Resolving Conflict Creatively Program (RCCP) for Educators for Social Responsibility. The program helps to foster better skills in conflict resolution and intergroup relations. (See chapter 1 and chapter 6 for more information on the RCCP.)

Lantieri holds a master's degree in elementary education and curriculum development from Hunter College and certificates of competency from the New York City Board of Education as a curriculum specialist and staff development specialist. She has more than 25 years of experience in education as a teacher, assistant principal, and director of an alternative middle school in East Harlem. She also served on the full-time education faculty of Hunter College for five years. From 1985 until the summer of 1993, she coordinated the RCCP for the New York City public schools.

Lantieri's work with youngsters was highlighted in a WCBS special, "Names *Can* Really Hurt Us," which was nominated for a local Emmy Award for best children's program in 1989. The RCCP was also highlighted on the prime-time network special "Kids Killing Kids/Kids Saving Kids," which received the 1994 National Emmy Award for best children's program. She is the executive producer of several videos, including *Waging Peace in Our Schools* (February 1993), a recent production about the RCCP's work around the country, and "Beginning with the Children: A National Teleconference on Violence Prevention" (March 1993), which linked four cities and aired in March 1993 on WNYE-TV, New York.

In 1993, Lantieri received the Richard R. Green Distinguished Educator Award for Fostering Intergroup Relations presented by the Anti-Defamation League. She is coauthor with Janet Patti of *Waging Peace in Our Schools* (1996).

William Modzeleski

William Modzeleski has more than 20 years of experience at the local and federal levels in criminal and juvenile justice. He is currently director of the U.S. Department of Education's Safe and Drug-Free Schools Program. In this role, he designs and develops drug and alcohol prevention programs and school violence prevention programs and activities. He helped design the Safe Schools Act of 1994, which provided assistance to local educational agencies for violence prevention activities. He was also instrumental in the reauthorization of the Safe and Drug-Free Schools and Communities Act of 1994.

Prior to his current position, Modzeleski served as executive director of the National Commission on Drug-Free Schools. He also served on the Attorney General's Task Force on Family Violence, the President's Child Safety Partnership, and the commission for the White House Conference for a Drug-Free America.

While at the Department of Justice, Modzeleski served in a variety of capacities, including juvenile justice and corrections specialist, staff director of the Coordinating Council on Juvenile Justice and Delinquency Prevention, director of Family Violence Programs, and federal coordinator of the High-Impact Cities Program in Newark, New Jersey.

Modzeleski has served on numerous interagency task forces at the Department of Justice and the Department of Education. Most recently he served on the Interagency Working Group on Violence Prevention (he chaired the School Violence Prevention Subgroup and cochaired the Youth Development Subgroup), on the Pulling America's Communities Together (PACT) steering committee, and on the Partnerships against Violence Network (PAVNET) steering committee. He also helped design the first and second interagency forums on youth violence prevention.

Deborah B. Prothrow-Stith (b. 1964)

Deborah B. Prothrow-Stith is a nationally recognized public health leader with applied and academic experience ranging from neighborhood clinics and inner-city hospitals, to serving as state commissioner of health, to being a dean and professor at the Harvard School of Public Health. She received a bachelor of arts degree in mathematics at Spelman College in 1975 and a medical degree from Harvard Medical School in 1979. She trained in internal medicine at Boston City Hospital.

Appointed in 1987 as the first woman and youngest commissioner of public health for the Commonwealth of Massachusetts, Prothrow-Stith expanded treatment programs for AIDS and drug rehabilitation and provided leadership on such health issues as environmental health, tuberculosis, immunizations, resource allocations for construction of new hospitals, and criteria for utilization of new health care technologies. During her tenure, she established the first office of violence prevention in a department of public health.

Prothrow-Stith's interest in violence prevention was stimulated by her work as a resident at Boston City Hospital. The typical "stitch them up, send them out" medical response to patients injured by violence led to her examination of violence as a social disease that could be prevented through public health strategies. She developed and wrote the first violence prevention curriculum for schools and communities, entitled "Violence Prevention Curriculum for Adolescents," and cowrote *Deadly Consequences*, the first book to present the public health perspective on violence to a mass audience.

As a chief spokesperson for a national movement to prevent violence, Prothrow-Stith supports the application of rigorous scientific methods to violence prevention programs, the expansion of public knowledge, and the strengthening of local, state, and federal programs for violence prevention. Her ability to articulate and advocate for the public health perspective has led to numerous appearances and requests for her participation on national media and public forums. She has authored or coauthored more than 40 publications on medical and public health issues. She is coauthor of a textbook entitled *Health Skills for Wellness* published by Prentice-Hall—the first high school health textbook to include an entire chapter devoted exclusively to preventing violence.

The Harvard School of Public Health hired Prothrow-Stith as assistant dean for Government and Community Programs in response to the Institute of Medicine's critique of schools of public health in the "Future of Public Health," which outlined a need to bridge the gap between academic public health and public health practice. At the Harvard School of Public Health, she has been a principal investigator on research grants, an active participant in the school's Injury Control Center, and was appointed professor for a new initiative, Public Health Practice.

Prothrow-Stith's current projects continue to reflect her dedication to adolescent violence prevention. The Community Violence Prevention Project, which is dedicated to increasing the knowledge base around issues of violence prevention for five major audiences—program operators, grantmakers, educators, policymakers, and community leaders—has developed a user-friendly how-to guide that will provide a point of departure for establishing antiviolence programs in communities. This work, entitled *Peace by Piece: A Guide to Preventing Community Violence*, is based on the experiences of more than 40 exemplary programs from across the country and presents more than 50 violence prevention-related activities.

Another project under Prothrow-Stith's direction focuses on the Neighborhood Health Center. In this setting, a pilot program has been initiated where a violence prevention counselor is on staff and is able to meet with and/or refer to appropriate agencies adolescents involved in violent situations as victims, witnesses, or perpetrators. This project is currently expanding to include training for health care providers across the state.

For her outstanding contribution to a wide range of public health problems, Prothrow-Stith has received three honorary doctorate awards, the World Health Day Award in 1993, and the Secretary of Health and Human Services Award in 1989.

Richard W. Riley (b. 1933)

U.S. Secretary of Education Richard Wilson Riley has been praised widely for his role in recent U.S. education reform. His nomination in December 1992 received unequivocal support; he was unanimously confirmed a month later following President Bill Clinton's inauguration.

Clinton chose Riley for the post of secretary of education so that Riley could help work the same kind of education reform on a national scale that he did as a two-term governor of South Carolina. There he spearheaded a highly successful reform of that state's school system by bringing together a coalition of businesspeople, educators, and parents.

Indeed, Riley's work as secretary of education has been admirable. In the first 21 months of the Clinton administration, due in large part to Riley's efforts and his ability to build bipartisan coalitions, Clinton signed into law six groundbreaking education initiatives. These included the Gun-Free Schools Act of 1994 and the Safe and Drug-Free Schools and Communities Act of 1994.

Riley was born in Greenville County, South Carolina. He graduated cum laude from Furman University in 1954 and served for two years as an officer on a minesweeper in the U.S. Navy. In 1959 Riley received a law degree from the University of South Carolina School of Law. He served as legal counsel to the Judiciary Committee of the U.S. Senate, and as a South Carolina state representative and state senator from 1963 to 1977. Riley was elected governor of South Carolina in 1978. He was reelected in 1982, after the people of South Carolina voted to amend the state constitution to enable him to be the first person in South Carolina history to run for a second term.

Ronald D. Stephens (b. 1946)

Ronald D. Stephens currently serves as executive director of the National School Safety Center in Thousand Oaks, California, a national federal clearinghouse for school safety programs and activities related to campus security; school law; community relations; student discipline and attendance; and the prevention of drug abuse, gangs, and bullying.

His past experience includes service as a teacher, assistant superintendent, and school board member. His administrative duties have included serving as a chief school business officer and as vice-president of Pepperdine University. He holds undergraduate and graduate degrees in business management, a doctorate from the University of Southern California, a California teaching credential, an administrative credential, and the Certificate in School Business Management.

In addition to his work as executive director of the National School Safety Center, Stephens serves as a consultant and frequent speaker for school districts, law enforcement agencies, and professional organizations nationwide. He also serves as the executive editor of *School Safety*, the leading U.S. school crime prevention newsletter. He has appeared on every major television network to discuss violence prevention, including appearances on "The Today Show," "Good Morning America," and "Oprah."

Betty R. Yung (b. 1945)

Betty Yung is associate professor for the School of Professional Psychology at Wright State University and the director for the Center for Child and Adolescent Violence Prevention. She had a major programmatic role in the development of the Positive Adolescent Choices Training (PACT) program, a violence prevention initiative primarily directed at middle school-age African-American youth. She was also instrumental in establishing local and national training institutes to prepare practitioners from diverse disciplines to establish youth violence prevention programs.

Yung received her doctorate from the University of Kentucky. She was formerly grants specialist for the School of Professional Psychology and officer of grants, research, and evaluation for the College of Education and Human Services at Wright State University. Prior to that, she had ten years of experience in casework and administration of youth programming in a juvenile court setting.

Yung has served as a consultant for the Dayton public schools; the Montgomery County Alcohol, Drug Addiction, and Mental Health Services Board; the Miami Valley Child Development Center Head Start Programs; the Children's Medical Center; and the Ohio Commission on Minority Health on program and grant proposal development in a variety of health and education areas for children, adolescents, and young adults.

In 1994, Yung won a Gimbel Child and Family Scholars Award for Service and Scholarship in Violence Prevention. Also in 1994, she and her coauthor, Dr. Rodney Hammond, won the Society for Research on Adolescents' "Best Journal Article on Adolescent Social Policy" award for their *American Psychologist* article on psychology's role in the public health response to assaultive violence among young African-American men.

Educational, Technological, and Regulatory Approaches

Federal Legislation

The Gun-Free Schools Act of 1994

The Gun-Free Schools Act (GFSA) is Title XIV of the Elementary and Secondary Education Act of 1965 (ESEA), which was reauthorized in 1994 as the Improving America's Schools Act. Under the GFSA, each state receiving ESEA funds must have a state law that requires a local educational agency (LEA) to expel from school for not less than one year any student who brings a firearm to school. The LEA's chief administering officer may modify the expulsion requirement on a case-by-case basis. The act does not amend or create an exception to federal civil rights laws. Thus, school districts must comply with:

Nondiscrimination requirements of Title VI of the Civil Rights Act of 1964, which prohibits discrimination on the basis of race, color, or national origin

Title IX of the Education Act of 1972, which prohibits discrimination on the basis of gender

Section 504 of the Rehabilitation Act of 1973, Title II of the Americans with Disabilities Act, which prohibits discrimination on the basis of disability

The Age Discrimination Act of 1975, which prohibits discrimination on the basis of age

Whether a child's behavior is caused by a disability must be determined through a reevaluation by individuals personally familiar with him or her and knowledgeable about special education. Educational services must continue for students with disabilities who are properly expelled, although the services may be provided in another setting. If the student's action in bringing a firearm to school is related to his or her disability, the student may not be expelled but may instead be suspended for up to ten days. The LEA may also seek a court order to remove a student who is considered dangerous.

Private schools are not subject to the provisions of the GFSA. However, private school students who participate in LEA programs or activities are subject to the one-year expulsion requirement.

The Safe and Drug-Free Schools and Communities Act of 1994

The Safe and Drug-Free Schools and Communities Act (SDFSCA), Title IV of the Improving America's Schools Act of 1994, authorizes the secretary of education to make grants to states to prevent school violence and to deter the use of illegal drugs and alcohol. Formerly called the Drug-Free Schools and Communities Act of 1987, this authorization includes violence prevention as a key program element.

The SDFSCA provides federal assistance to governors, state and local educational agencies, institutions of higher education, and nonprofit entities for:

Grants to LEAs and educational service agencies to establish, operate, and improve local programs of school drug and violence prevention, early intervention, rehabilitation referral, and education in elementary and secondary schools

Grants to public and private community-based agencies and organizations for programs of drug and violence prevention, early intervention, rehabilitation referral, and education

Development, training, technical assistance, and coordination activities

Allowable activities include violence prevention and education programs for students, training and technical assistance for teachers, and developing violence and drug prevention programs that involve parents and coordination with the community.

A national evaluation system is now being established to assess the impact of the SDFSCA on youth, schools, and communities. To encourage community-wide strategies, LEAs must develop their drug and violence prevention plans in cooperation with local government, businesses, parents, medical and law enforcement professionals, and community-based organizations.

The Violent Crime Control and Law Enforcement Act of 1994

The Violent Crime Control and Law Enforcement Act of 1994 authorized $30.2 billion, including $7 billion for initiatives in "crime prevention," aimed at keeping youth crime free. It put more police officers on the streets, funded new prison construction, imposed stiffer penalties on violent crime (including a mandatory term of life in prison for offenders with three or more convictions for serious, violent felonies and drug-trafficking charges), and banned deadly assault weapons. The act also expanded federal assistance for community-based crime prevention efforts, including programs and activities that help improve opportunities for youth—especially youth in poor and high-crime areas.

Goals 2000: Educate America Act of 1994

The Goals 2000: Educate America Act of 1994 provides resources to states and communities to develop and implement education reforms that will help students reach academic and occupational standards. The original six goals were developed by the nation's governors in 1989 when they committed themselves to a nationwide educational reform effort. These six goals, with the addition of two more, were formalized into law with the passage of the Goals 2000: Educate America Act. Listed below are the eight National Education Goals.

Goal 1: Ready To Learn

By the year 2000, all children in the United States will start school ready to learn.

Goal 2: School Completion

By the year 2000, the high school graduation rate will increase to at least 90 percent.

Goal 3: Student Achievement and Citizenship

By the year 2000, all students will leave grades 4, 8, and 12 having demonstrated competency over challenging subject matter, including English, mathematics, science, foreign languages, civics and government, economics, arts, history, and geography. Every school in the United States will ensure that all students learn to use their minds well, so they may be prepared for responsible citizenship, further learning, and productive employment in the economy.

Goal 4: Teacher Education and Professional Development

By the year 2000, the nation's teaching force will have access to programs for the continued improvement of their professional skills and the opportunity to acquire the knowledge and skills needed to instruct and prepare all students in the United States for the next century.

Goal 5: Mathematics and Science

By the year 2000, students in the United States will be first in the world in mathematics and science achievement.

Goal 6: Adult Literacy and Lifelong Learning

By the year 2000, every adult in the United States will be literate and will possess the knowledge and skills necessary to compete in a global economy and exercise the rights and responsibilities of citizenship.

Goal 7: Safe, Disciplined, and Alcohol- and Drug-Free Schools

By the year 2000, every school in the United States will be free of drugs, violence, and the unauthorized presence of firearms and alcohol and will offer a disciplined environment conducive to learning.

Goal 8: Parental Participation

By the year 2000, every school in the United States will promote partnerships that will increase parental involvement and participation in promoting the social, emotional, and academic growth of children.

Telecommunications Bill of 1996

Passed in July 1996, this controversial bill—the first major rewrite of communications law since the Communications Act of 1934—significantly alters telecommunications regulation. First, it eliminates regulatory barriers in long-distance, local telephone, and cable markets. Local telephone companies now have the right to compete with long-distance carriers to offer long-distance services. Cable services no longer face rate regulation for their basic services. And broadcast owners may now own a cable system and a broadcast outlet in the same city. Second, this bill censors material deemed indecent on the Internet and imposes prison terms and fines on those who make indecent material available over computer networks.

An amendment to the Telecommunications Bill requires television manufacturers to include a V-chip or comparable technology in every television set with a 13-inch or larger screen. The V-chip, which in reality is a close-captioned controller that can be implemented in software, allows parents to block violent programming.

An outgrowth of the Telecommunications Bill, a six-tier television program rating system that was developed by a board of broadcast executives, began implementation in January 1997. Similar to the motion picture rating system, it rates programs as TV-Y (suitable for all children), TV-Y7 (for children ages 7 and above), TV-G (for all audiences, TV-PG (parental guidance suggested), TV-14 (not suitable for children under 14), and TV-M (for mature audiences only). Some decry this system as inadequate and assert that ratings should describe the violence, adult language, and sexual content in television programming.

Because of the controversy over the current rating system, which will be in place for a ten-month trial period, along with required procedures such as Federal Communications Commission (FCC) approval, it will take years before the V-chip becomes a functioning component of television sets. In 1997

Congress and the FCC will hold hearings to discuss the rating system. If they decide it does not go far enough, the FCC will devise its own system.

Statewide Approaches to Violence Prevention

To gather information for this section, each state department of education in the United States was queried for information on its educational, technological, and regulatory approaches to school violence prevention, along with the titles of available publications and research studies. Twenty-three of our 50 states—46 percent—reported. For those states that did not report, the names and addresses of their Safe and Drug-Free Schools coordinators are listed.

Alabama

Approaches to School Violence Prevention

Alabama only adopts state-developed curriculums. The Safe and Drug-Free Schools Program has provided funding for training to faculties and school systems statewide, mainly from a violence prevention series entitled *Freedom from Violence,* published by the Altschul Group Corporation.

Recent state legislation mandated that all local boards of education develop and implement a character education program for all grades to consist of not less than ten minutes of daily instruction focusing on the students' development of 25 key character traits. Each program must include the Pledge of Allegiance to the U.S. flag. Character traits are correlated with objectives from Alabama's courses of study and with the essential skills composing the state's counseling program. The Alabama State Department of Education plans to survey local education agencies (LEAs) to determine the level of character education implementation and the establishment of a database for character education exchange instruction.

There have been various joint educational school violence prevention efforts with city police departments throughout the state. A percentage of the Safe and Drug-Free Schools and Communities funds has been allocated to the Alabama Governor's Office for law enforcement activities; the state has chosen to fund Drug Abuse Resistance Education (DARE) grants. Law enforcement agencies also collaborate with community advisory councils that direct and plan drug and violence prevention programs in their communities. Law enforcement agencies also provide resources officers, who serve one-year assignments in many Alabama schools.

Alabama has been implementing peer-helping programs since the 1970s. The First Annual Peer Sponsor Conference was held in February 1996 and nationally known presenters discussed peer helping, peer tutoring, peer mediation, and peer ministry. Statewide conferences have been held for the past several years to train peer-helper teams of students and sponsors.

Each LEA that receives Safe and Drug-Free Schools and Communities funds is monitored by the Alabama State Department of Education every other year for compliance with federal and state laws.

With respect to technological and environmental interventions, a safe schools packet was sent to each LEA that included a safe schools checklist, a sample disciplinary code, and a copy of all updated laws. Metal detectors, uniforms, identification cards, and a visitor registration process are all used as interventions/methods of protection. "Safe and Drug-Free Zone" and "Weapon-Free Zone" signs are posted throughout many school systems in the state.

The Alabama State Department of Education has developed and disseminated sample policies for LEAs with respect to:

Television surveillance cameras

Student dress code

Metal detectors

Fighting

School safety and security committee

School resource officers and school security personnel

A notification policy addressing parents' potential civil and criminal liabilities for misbehavior by a student on school property or against school employees

Evaluations of school violence prevention efforts are conducted at the conclusion of each student activity and teacher training session. The Alabama State Department of Education offers follow-up technical assistance and revitalization training.

Significant State Legislation

All local boards of education in the state of Alabama are accountable for compliance with statutes and regulations regarding school safety and discipline. If a local board of education is determined to have failed in its compliance, after one year the state superintendent of education will assume direct management. By legislative mandate, the Alabama State Department of Education must annually send to all local boards of education and all local superintendents of education a manual containing all acts of the legislature and all state board of education regulations that pertain to school safety and discipline.

Alabama legislatively mandates the expulsion of students for a period of one year if they have brought to school or have in their possession a firearm in school buildings, on school grounds, on school buses, or at other school-sponsored functions.

School officials, district attorneys, juvenile court judges, juvenile probation officers, and other agencies and organizations are collaborating to implement laws and regulations that address school violence. The School Conduct Intervention Program, designed to inform students and families of school conduct expectations, sanctions, and procedures, is an example of such collaboration.

Teacher Assault, Ala. Code §16-1-24 (1975). A person commits the crime of assault in the second degree (Class C felony) if the person assaults with intent to cause serious physical injury to a teacher or an employee of a public educational institution during or as a result of the performance of his or her duty.

Drugs, Alcohol, Weapons, Physical Harm, or Threatened Physical Harm, Ala. Code §16-1-24.2, §16-1-24.1 (1975). The school principal shall notify appropriate law enforcement officials when a person violates local board of education policies concerning drugs, alcohol, weapons, physical harm to a person, or threatened physical harm to a person. If any criminal charge is warranted, the principal is authorized to sign the appropriate warrant. If that person is a student, the local school system shall immediately suspend that person from attending regular classes and schedule a hearing within five school days.

If a person is found to have violated a local board of education policy concerning drugs, alcohol, weapons, physical harm to a person or threatened physical harm, the person may not be readmitted to the public schools until criminal charges have been disposed of by appropriate authorities and the person has satisfied all other requirements imposed by the local board of education as a condition for readmission.

Weapons in Schools, Ala. Code §13-A-11-72 (1975).

No person shall knowingly with intent to do bodily harm carry or possess a deadly weapon on the premises of a public school. Doing so is a Class C felony. The term "deadly weapon" means a firearm or anything designed, made, or adapted for the purpose of inflicting death or serious physical injury.

Vandalism, Ala. Code §6-5-380 (1975).

The parents, guardian, or other person having control of any minor under the age of 18 with whom the minor is living and who have custody of the minor are liable for the actual damages sustained to school property, plus the court costs, caused by the minor's intentional, willful, or malicious act.

Pistol Possession/Driver's License, Ala. Code §16-28-40 (1975).

Any person over age 14 who is convicted of the crime of possession of a pistol on the premises of a public school, or a public school bus, shall be denied issuance of a driver's permit or license to operate a motor vehicle for 180 days from the date the person is eligible and applies for a permit or license. If a person over age 14 possesses a driver's license on the date of conviction, the driver's license will be suspended for 180 days.

State Department of Education Resources

It's the Law! Parental Notification of Civil Liabilities and Criminal Penalties

Lists the laws that relate to civil liabilities and criminal penalties for violence or other misbehavior by students on school property or against school employees.

Manual of Laws and Regulations Pertaining to School Safety and Discipline, October 20, 1995

Contains acts passed by the Alabama state legislature during 1995 and regulations adopted by the state board of education during the 1994–1995 school year in the areas of school safety and discipline.

Discipline Plan for Safe Schools, July 1995

Provides local boards of education with guidance in developing their discipline plans—the policies, practices, and procedures that govern the behavior of students, staff, parents, and others who have access to school campuses, property, and events.

School Conduct Intervention Program (Implementing the Parental Responsibility Statute Ala. Code §16-28-12, 1975), July 1995

Outlines the roles and responsibilities of parents, schools, and the courts in school conduct intervention.

State Contact

Penny Deavers, Safe and Drug-Free Schools and Communities
  Act Education Specialist
    Alabama Department of Education
    Gordon Persons Building
    P.O. Box 302101
    Montgomery, Alabama 36130-2101
    (334) 242-8049

Alaska

State Contact

Helen Mehrkens
    Education Administration
    Alaska Department of Education
    Drug-Free Schools Program
    801 West 10th Street, Suite 200
    Juneau, AK 99801-1894
    (907) 465-8730
    (907) 465-2713 (FAX)

Arizona

State Contact

Chris McIntier
    Student Services Team Leader
    Title IV—Safe & Drug-Free Schools
    Arizona Department of Education
    1535 West Jefferson
    Phoenix, AZ 85007
    (602) 542-8728
    (602) 542-3818 (FAX)
    colson@macpo.ade.state.az.us

Arkansas

State Contact

Otistene Smith
Drug Education Program Adviser
Arkansas Department of Education
#4 Capitol Mall, 405B
Little Rock, AR 72201-1071
(501) 682-5170
(501) 682-4618 (FAX)

California

Approaches to School Violence Prevention

Since 1983, the California state superintendent of public instruction and the state attorney general have unified their efforts and resources through the School/Law Enforcement (S/LE) Partnership, which promotes programs that enhance the safety of California schools. The Partnership highlights programs such as conflict resolution, peer mediation, character education, and gang violence reduction through its annual conference. It provides technical assistance on school safety through its Cadre members—100 professionals from law enforcement, education, and other agencies that serve youth. The Partnership also sponsors regional training of safe school planning processes and community mobilization for the development of strategic approaches for safer schools and communities.

School violence prevention activities in the state of California include mentoring, school dress codes, comprehensive health education, community service, hate-motivated violence prevention, coordinated family service delivery models, and school security personnel and hardware with strong collaboration between the School Safety and Violence Prevention Office and the Healthy Kids, Healthy California Office. The state Department of Education is working with the California legislature to identify funding for schools, districts, and county offices of education for conflict resolution and peer mediation programs.

Alternative education programs provide education options to students for the purpose of continuing and completing their education. These programs offer opportunities for students and their families to redefine the importance of school, encourage parental involvement in development of student behavior, and motivate students to change inappropriate conduct such as truancy or violent behavior.

In July 1995, the California Safe Schools Assessment began collecting school crime data from school districts and county offices of education. The data provides the legislature with a comprehensive understanding of the most pressing crime and safety issues confronting students, teachers, administrators, and community members in their local schools; measures the safety needs of schools and students; provides the basis for decisions on resource allocation; and establishes a priority direction for prevention programs to be funded at the state level.

Significant State Legislation

Crime and Violence on School Campuses: Grant Program, Senate Bill No. 1043. Extends appropriation of

funds for Section 32230 of the Education Code, which established the Conflict Resolution and School Violence Reduction Program, until 1 January 2000. This statewide grant program is coordinated through county offices of education and provides grants to schools for conflict resolution projects.

According to Senate Bill 1043, the superintendent of public instruction must contract for an ongoing independent evaluation of the effectiveness of conflict resolution projects funded by grants. The evaluation is to determine the effectiveness of each conflict resolution project where it is conducted, based on these criteria:

> Reduction in incidents of school violence at the school site
>
> Reduction in the number of suspensions or expulsions of pupils for violent behavior at the school site
>
> A comparison of incidents of school violence with schools of similar size and pupils of similar socioeconomic background

On or before 1 June 1998, the superintendent will submit to the legislature an interim progress report. On or before 1 October 1999, the superintendent will submit to the legislature a final evaluation report, both of which shall be based on the ongoing evaluation.

Schools: Dress Codes: Uniforms, Senate Bill No. 1269.

This bill authorizes the governing board of a school district to adopt or rescind a reasonable dress code policy that requires students to wear a schoolwide uniform or prohibits them from wearing "gang-related apparel" if the governing board determines that the policy is necessary for the health and safety of the school environment. If a schoolwide uniform is required, the specific uniform would be selected by the principal, staff, and parents of the individual school.

Sections of the California Education Code Dealing with Expulsion

Current California law authorizes governing boards to expel students for specified offenses, and categorizes the offenses by degree of seriousness and the corresponding amount of discretion governing boards have in responding to them. There are three categories of offenses:

> Less serious offenses for which the governing board may expel a student (Section 48900), including possession of an imitation (replica) of a firearm that would lead a reasonable person to believe it was real

> More serious offenses for which the principal or superintendent must recommend expulsion unless mitigating circumstances exist and the governing board may choose not to expel the student (Section 48915), including causing serious injury to another, possessing a knife or other dangerous object, unlawfully possessing drugs, and robbery or extortion

> Mandatory offenses for which the principal or superintendent must immediately suspend and recommend expulsion and the governing board must expel the student if the offense occurred (Section 48915), including possessing, selling, or furnishing a firearm; brandishing a knife at another person; or unlawfully selling a controlled substance

Additional sections of the code provide for expulsion options such as community service, expulsion requirements (for example, length, rehabilitation plans for expelled students, program of study referrals, expulsion placements, readmission of expelled students), alternative educational placement, and reporting and evaluation requirements.

State Department of Education Resources

Safe Schools: A Planning Guide for Action, 1995 ed.

Shows schools how to form partnerships with law enforcement agencies and the community to develop a safe school plan that includes the whole school environment. Designed to be used in conjunction with the Office of the California Attorney General's publication *Law in the School*, which provides a comprehensive look at statutory and case law relating to schools and their surrounding communities. Includes a seven-step safe school planning process that is recommended in implementing safe school strategies.

Handbook on the Rights and Responsibilities of School Personnel and Students in the Areas Providing Moral, Civic, and Ethical Education, Teaching about Religion, Promoting Responsible Attitudes and Behaviors, and Preventing and Responding to Hate Violence

A resource for teachers, school administrators, board members, and parents that offers information on what can and should be taught about religion, civic values, ethics, manners, democratic principles, responsible attitudes and behaviors, and preventing and responding to hate and violence.

State Contact

Karen Lowrey, Consultant
    School Safety and Violence Prevention Office
    Department of Education
    560 J Street, Suite 260
    Sacramento, CA 95814
    (916) 323-1027
    (916) 323-6061 (FAX)
    klowrey@cde.ca.gov

Colorado

State Contact

Kathie Jackson, Program Director
    Colorado Department of Education
    Prevention Initiatives Unit
    201 East Colfax Avenue
    Denver, CO 80203
    (303) 866-6869
    (303) 830-0793 (FAX)

Connecticut

State Contact

Nancy Letney Pugliese
    Education Consultant
    Connecticut Department of Education
    P.O. Box 2219, Room G-32
    Hartford, CT 06145-2219
    (203) 566-6645
    (203) 566-5623 (FAX)

Delaware

Approaches to School Violence Prevention

Approaches employed throughout the state of Delaware include counseling; discipline with dignity; conflict, dispute, and crisis resolution; anger control; time-out opportunities; in-school suspension; after-school detention; tutoring services; security guards; Saturday school; study skills programs; parenting skills programs; and drug abuse prevention programs.

Significant State Legislation

HB 85. Signed into law in 1993, HB 85 requires that evidence of certain incidents of student conduct in Delaware schools be reported to the superintendent of public instruction and to the Youth Division of the Delaware State Police. Such incidents include assault against a pupil, extortion against a pupil, assault against a school employee, extortion against a school employee, offensive touching against a school employee, terroristic threatening against a school employee, possession of a dangerous instrument or deadly weapon by a pupil, and possession of an unlawful controlled substance by a pupil.

HB 247. Enacted in 1994, HB 247 established a statewide program to improve student behavior and thus provide for a safe school climate. The program provides for the treatment of pupils who exhibit serious discipline problems and for the establishment of services to children that will reduce the severity of disruptive behavior in the future. The law has three components:

> Creation of alternative settings for disruptive students whose behavior makes recommendation for expulsion imminent or whose behavior results in expulsion

> Support for school-based intervention programs

Establishment of community-based partnerships with such organizations as the Department of Health and Social Services

The bill also authorizes the Governor's Family Services Cabinet Council to fund local school/community projects that focus on preventing discipline problems in Delaware schools before they occur. Prevention programs might include such facets as academic tutoring and student mentoring programs, outreach efforts to promote parent and community involvement, and training to help students and staff resolve conflicts.

HB 281. This law expands the school-based intervention component of HB 247 to provide resources to kindergarten through grade 12. The legislation significantly increases potential grant awards for grades seven through ten in schools that establish site-based decision-making committees to govern school discipline matters.

HB 171. HB 171 provides for criminal charges and more severe penalties for anyone possessing a weapon within 1,000 feet of any school building, athletic field, sports stadium, or any vehicle owned, operated, or leased by any public or private school, including any college or university. Also included are community recreation centers, athletic fields, and stadiums. If the perpetrator is a student, he or she will be expelled for 180 school days.

State Department of Education Resources

Overview of Statewide Task Force on Discipline, HB 85, HB 247, HB 171, HB 281, HB 284, Department of Public Instruction, Comprehensive School Discipline Improvement

Encapsulates the significant state legislation discussed above.

Alternative School Programs, Comprehensive School Discipline Improvement, January 1995

Describes alternative school programs whose goal is to reduce the incidence and impact of delinquent behavior on the youth of three counties in Delaware: the "Because We Care" Alternative Education Program and the "PEAK Program for Educational Alternatives" in Kent County; "New Beginnings" in New Castle County; and the Sussex County Secondary Alternative School.

School-Based Intervention Programs, Comprehensive School Discipline Improvement

Discusses the school-based intervention programs implemented from kindergarten through grade 12 in the following school districts: Appoquinimink, Brandywine, Caesar Rodney, Cape Henlopen, Capital, Christina, Colonial, Delmar, Indian River, Lake Forest, Laurel, Milford, New Castle County Vocational Technical, Polytech, Red Clay Consolidated, Seaford, Smyrna, Sussex Tech, and Woodbridge.

School and Community Partnerships Prevention Programs, Comprehensive School Discipline Improvement

Describes the purpose and design of community school violence prevention partnerships in the following school districts: Cape Henlopen, Seaford, Woodbridge, Laurel, and Christina.

State Contact

Ronald A. Meade, Education Associate
    Student/Family/School Support Team
    Improvements & Assistance Branch
    Delaware Department of Public Instruction
    Townsend Building
    Dover, DE 19903-1402
    (302) 739-4676
    (302) 739-3744 (FAX)
    MEADE@bach.udel.edu

District of Columbia

State Contact

Essie G. Page
    Brown Administration Unit
    26th Street & Benning Road, NE
    Washington, DC 20004
    (202) 724-4178
    (202) 727-1516 (FAX)

Florida

Approaches to School Violence Prevention

Florida is now broadening its focus to include violence prevention and school safety in its safe and drug-free school efforts. Violence prevention activities in 1996 included a curriculum review criteria update to include sections on violence prevention and integration with broader prevention strategies.

Florida has put considerable effort into its campaign to heighten awareness and reduce student use of alcohol, tobacco, and other drugs. Local safe and drug-free schools efforts emphasize classroom instruction and awareness campaigns. Elementary and middle school curriculums include skill-building instruction on resistance, communication, and conflict resolution. At the middle school and high school levels, many districts conduct peer-based efforts that teach communication and mediation skills. Although most districts use commercially developed prevention curricula, some districts have found it more cost effective to develop their own.

Many Florida schools offer Student Assistance Programs (SAPs) made up of school staff members who identify, assess, and refer for treatment students with problems that affect their schoolwork. SAP responses include a variety of intervention strategies. SAPs are used at all school levels and are coupled with peer-based efforts. Interventions may be simple (for example, developing a temporary staff buddy for an elementary student who is getting into fights) or intense. SAPs offer reentry activities for those students returning from treatment for alcohol, tobacco, or other drug use.

In 1994–1995, to determine the effectiveness of its safe and drug-free school efforts, many districts administered student surveys on alcohol, tobacco, and other drug use, or conducted pre- and post-tests to determine effectiveness of classroom instruction. Some districts tracked discipline referrals as well as alcohol/tobacco/other drug district policy violations resulting in suspensions or expulsions. Some districts determined effectiveness by a lower dropout rate or a drop in the number of juvenile arrests. A few districts determined effectiveness if the number of drug- and alcohol-related emergency room cases for juveniles decreased.

Many districts conducted a baseline survey to use for future surveys. Pre- and post-tests administered around the state to determine effectiveness of classroom instruction overall indicated that students were gaining more knowledge about drug prevention and violence prevention issues.

State Department of Education Resources

Achieving Goal Five: Assessment and Planning Guide for Goal Five of Blueprint 2000

Blueprint 2000 is Florida's plan for school reform and accountability. This guide is designed to help schools and districts achieve Goal Five of Blueprint 2000, which deals with school safety and environment, by assessing their current status and developing a school improvement plan.

Florida Safe and Drug-Free Schools Program State Report for 1994–95
Reports on the state's safe and drug-free efforts during 1994–1995.

Hot Topics: Usable Research: Alternatives to Suspension
Provides ideas about alternative disciplinary interventions as well as prevention strategies that can reduce disciplinary problems. (For more information, contact the Prevention Center, Florida Department of Education.)

State Contact
John R. "Skip" Forsyth, Program Director
    Safe and Drug-Free Schools Program
    Florida Department of Education
    325 West Gaines Street, Suite 3322
    Tallahassee, FL 32399-0400
    (904) 488-6304
    (904) 488-6319 (FAX)

Georgia

State Contact
Sandi Denham, Coordinator
    Health & Physical Education
    Georgia Department of Education
    1952 Twin Towers East
    Atlanta, GA 30334-5040
    (404) 651-9406
    (404) 651-8582 (FAX)

Hawaii

State Contact
Kendyl Ko
    State Health Education Specialist
    Safe and Drug-Free Schools
    Department of Education
    General Education Branch
    189 Lunalilo Home Road, 2nd Floor

Honolulu, HI 96825
(808) 396-2563
(808) 548-5390 (FAX)

Idaho

State Contact
Patricia G. Getty
Drug Education Consultant
Idaho Department of Education
650 West State Street
Len B. Jordan Building
Boise, ID 83720
(208) 334-5132
(208) 334-2229 (FAX)

Illinois

Approaches to School Violence Prevention
At present, the Illinois State Board of Education does not involve itself in statewide curriculum planning. Thus, local school districts are not mandated to adopt specific curriculum in conflict resolution or character education. However, school districts are required to provide violence prevention and conflict resolution education for grades 4 through 12, provided the program can be exclusively funded by grants from private sources or the federal government.

Pursuant to the determination of need through a public hearing, each regional superintendent must decide whether to establish an alternative school for disruptive students who are defined as "suspension or expulsion eligible." Disruptive students transferred to an alternative school must be provided with an alternative education plan.

Various statewide educational resources include the following organizations and programs:

The Drug Awareness and Resistance Education Program (DARE), which focuses on developing life skills that will prevent a student's involvement with prohibited substances

The Violence Education and Gang Awareness Program (VEGA), an educational program that supplements DARE and is meant to reduce and prevent gang involvement and violence among young people

The Community Block Home Program, which provides a universal sign that would designate approved homes to which children can run in case of danger en route to and from school

The Illinois Council for the Prevention of Violence, which initiates and coordinates violence prevention efforts (for example, it publishes a violence prevention newsletter, etc.)

The Illinois Institute for Dispute Resolution, which pro-vides training and consultation regarding dispute resolu-tion, primarily focusing on building the capacity of local school staff and students to resolve their conflicts and avoid violence

The state Board of Education, in cooperation with various organizations, helps to sponsor and/or conduct confer-ences and workshops related to violence prevention, including the Safe and Drug-Free Schools Conference

The major organizations that represent local school dis-tricts and education (for example, the Illinois Association of School Boards) include violence-related information, training, and resources for their members

The Illinois Council for the Prevention of Violence conducts research (with some financial support from the state Board of Education) to evaluate the effectiveness of the state's school-based violence prevention programs.

Significant State Legislation

Students are prohibited from using or possessing electronic signaling and cellular radio-telecommunication devices, unless authorized by the building principal. Electronic signaling devices include pocket pagers and all similar electronic paging devices.

No one may distribute or deliver written or printed solicita-tions on school property, or within 1,000 feet of school property, for the purpose of inviting students to any event when a signifi-cant purpose of the event is to commit illegal acts or to solicit attendees to commit illegal acts. (This is an antigang measure.) Students may not bring weapons to school.

Local school boards must establish and maintain a parent-teacher advisory committee to develop guidelines on pupil discipline. Each committee, in cooperation with local law enforcement officials, must develop policies and procedures with the local school board to establish and maintain a reciprocal reporting system between the school district and local law enforcement officials regarding criminal offenses committed by students.

A school district's disciplinary policies must be distributed to students' parent(s) or guardian(s) within 15 days after the beginning of the school year, or within 15 days after starting classes for a student who transfers into the district during the school year. The district's students must also be informed of the contents of the disciplinary policies.

School officials may search students when there is reasonable suspicion of a violation of law or school rules; public property may be inspected by school officials pursuant to district policy.

School superintendents must notify local law enforcement officials when school staff complain of attacks and when students bring firearms or weapons to any school that receives federal funds. The Department of State Police must compile and report this information to the state Board of Education.

Local school boards must have a policy that provides for expulsion of a student who brings a weapon to school. The expulsion period is at least one year and up to two years; that time period may be modified by the board on a case-by-case basis. Local school boards may expel students guilty of gross disobedience or misconduct for up to two years; the specific period of time for the expulsion is determined on a case-by-case basis. Students may be suspended from school for up to ten days for gross disobedience or misconduct in school and/or suspended from riding the school bus for up to ten days for gross disobedience or misconduct on the school bus.

Corporal punishment may not be used in Illinois schools. However, school personnel may use reasonable force as needed to maintain safety for other students or school personnel, or for the purposes of self-defense or the defense of property.

State Department of Education Resources

Safe at School...A Public Promise: Recommendations for Restoring Safety and Order in Illinois Schools

Includes recommendations presented to the Illinois State Board of Education in December 1995 and adopted in January 1996 for violence prevention in Illinois schools.

State Contacts

Lee Patton, Executive Assistant to the State Board
    Illinois Board of Education
    100 North First Street
    Springfield, IL 62777-0001
    (217) 782-9560
    upatton@pr6.isbe.state.il.us

Myron Mason, Principal Consultant
    Illinois Board of Education
    100 North First Street
    Springfield, IL 62777-0001
    (217) 782-3810

Indiana

State Contact

Phyllis Lewis, Senior Officer
    Indiana Department of Education
    Center for School Improvement and Performance
    State House, Room 229
    Indianapolis, IN 46204-2798
    (317) 232-6984
    (317) 232-9121 (FAX)

Iowa

State Contact

David A. Wright
    Substance Education Consultant
    Iowa Department of Education
    Grimes State Office Building
    Des Moines, IA 50319
    (515) 281-3021
    (515) 242-6025 (FAX)

Kansas

Approaches to School Violence Prevention

Most of this state's work in preventing school violence is carried out at the district level. The state does not recommend specific conflict resolution curricula and programs or character education curricula. Staff members from the Kansas Department of Education work together to identify technical assistance that can be provided to schools attempting to help ensure a safer environment.

Evaluation factors used in determining a school's accredited status in this state are: (1) reduction of violent acts committed against students and staff and (2) maintenance of a low violence rate.

Significant State Legislation

Weapon-Free Schools, Chapter 72, Article 89a. Article 89a requires expulsion of pupils for possession of weapons at school. It was enacted to comply with the federal Gun-Free Schools Act of 1994.

School Safety and Security Act, Chapter 72, Article 89b. Article 89b requires an immediate report to be made to the appropriate state or local law enforcement agency by or on behalf of any school employee who knows or has reason to believe that a criminal act has been committed or will be committed, or that explosives, firearms, or weapons will be used at a school, on school property, or at a school-supervised activity. Such incidents must be compiled and reported annually to the state Board of Education. The board, in turn, must compile the reports and transmit them to the appropriate government personnel and agencies.

State Contact

Sharon E. Freden, Assistant Commissioner
    Learning Services Division
    Kansas Board of Education
    120 S.E. 10th Avenue
    Topeka, Kansas 66612-1182
    (913) 296-2303

Kentucky

Approaches to School Violence Prevention

Local school districts in Kentucky carry out this state's school violence prevention efforts. The "Be Against Drugs and Guns Entering Schools" (B.A.D.G.E.S.) program in Warren County is a partnership between local law enforcement agencies, schools, youth organizations, and parents. Law enforcement officers from nine community agencies enter schools and interact with students in a positive, supportive manner. Support is given for the development of a comprehensive antidrug, antiviolence program that includes teacher and staff training, parent education, student curricula, policy review and revision, youth service opportunities, and a variety of school and community awareness activities. The Safe Schools Program, also in Warren County schools, includes primary prevention efforts for all students, secondary prevention and early intervention efforts, and schoolwide plans for dealing with crisis.

In Franklin County public schools, middle school and high school teachers, counselors, and students are trained in a peer mediation/conflict resolution program to help students resolve their disputes and conflicts. The Redirection Center in Rowan County public schools serves students with severe disciplinary problems who otherwise would have been expelled. The Center follows strict physical and academic requirements similar to a military school.

The Volunteer Parent Patrols in Boyd County public schools provide security at extracurricular events. In Monroe County schools, all classrooms have telephones for immediate communication. And in Somerset Independent School District, videocameras are installed in hallways where lockers are located.

Significant State Legislation

Significant legislation in Kentucky that is directed at youth violence prevention includes:

> HB 312, which prohibits the unlawful possession of a weapon on school property

> HB 359, which prohibits persons under age 18 from possessing, manufacturing, or transporting a handgun

> HB 499, which requires primary program curricula to include preventing abduction and kidnapping

State Department of Education Resources

Student Safety Materials, Bowling Green City Schools

A report by the state's School Safety Committee that includes recommendations and acceptance of board policy changes, safety programs, guidelines, and a checklist for suspension/ expulsion of students, procedures for conducting disciplinary hearings, and notice to parents. (For more information, contact John C. Settle, 502-746-2200.)

State Contacts

Beverly L. Persley, Director
    Student/Family Support Services
    Kentucky Department of Education
    Capital Plaza Tower
    500 Mero Street
    Frankfort, KY 40601
    (502) 564-4770

Liz Storey, Student Assistance Coordinator
    B.A.D.G.E.S. Program (Warren County Schools)
    806 Kenton Street
    Bowling Green, KY 42101
    (502) 781-5150

Pat Guthrie, Assistant Superintendent for Student Services
    Safe Schools Program (Warren County Schools)
    806 Kenton Street
    Bowling Green, KY 42101
    (502) 781-5150

Joyce Peauce
    Peer Mediation: Conflict Resolution (Franklin County
    Public Schools)
    (502) 695-6750

Nadine Griffith
    Redirection Center (Rowan County Public Schools)
    (606) 784-8949

Louisiana

In 1993 the Louisiana Department of Education and the State Attorney General's Office formed a partnership to work for safe and drug-free schools. The result was a voluntary Safe School Recognition Program (SSRP) in which state and local education agencies jointly recognize individual schools that have voluntarily met the elements to be recognized as a "safe school"—that is, "an orderly and purposeful place where students and staff are free to learn and teach without the threat of physical and psychological harm." The program allows for voluntary involvement of schools and local communities to work together in order to identify strategies and develop and implement action plans to reduce school violence.

Participating schools complete the following steps:

Form a school building collaboration council

Receive training

Administer inventories on the personal characteristics of students and staff, the school physical plant and environment, the school and community social environment, and the school/community cultural environment

Conduct a self-study

Develop action plans

Implement action plans

Submit completed inventories, self-study, and action plans

Those schools that meet the state criteria are awarded safe school recognition. Local school boards determine appropriate recognition at the local level (for example, media coverage, awards, etc.).

State Contact
Dr. Moselle Dearbone
 Bureau of Student Services
 Louisiana Department of Education
 7th Floor
 P.O. Box 94064
 Baton Rouge, LA 70804-9004
 (504) 342-3480
 (504) 342-6887 (FAX)

Maine

Approaches to School Violence Prevention
In December 1995, Maine's Safe and Drug-Free Schools and Communities Task Force submitted a report to the state Department of Education outlining its recommendations for school violence prevention in the state. It offered a list of major recommendations to the legislature's Task Force on Learning Results, the educational system, policymakers, youth, families, and communities. What follows is a summary of the recommendations to each.

The Legislature and Task Force on Learning Results should:

Establish a statewide data collection system on illicit acts related to violence and substance abuse on school property and at school functions. This will provide information on youth health and development to the community and to decision makers in order to influence how resources are allocated statewide.

Develop, in collaboration with key agencies and groups, a set of conditions and factors by which local communities and their schools can measure progress toward being safe and drug-free.

Remove existing legal barriers that impede the sharing of critical information among all agencies that deal with youth at risk.

Provide and/or sustain adequate funding for youth drug/alcohol and violence prevention and maintenance programs.

Require that, as part of Maine's teacher and administrator preservice and recertification provisions, all persons receive specific training in development of successful classroom and school management skills, including skills that directly address prevention of youth violence and strategies for effectively responding to threats of violence and actual violence.

All Maine schools should:

Develop comprehensive prevention programs that address the needs of youth at risk

Develop and implement pre-kindergarten through grade 12 curricula and comprehensive prevention programming that would include diversity, tolerance, conflict resolution, sexual harassment, student peer mediation, and alcohol and drug abuse education

Policymakers should:

Develop policies to create safe and drug-free schools (weapons policies, harassment policies, etc.)

Establish a mandated, statewide data collection system on illicit acts related to issues of violence and substance abuse on school property and/or at school functions

Develop, in collaboration with key agencies and groups, a set of conditions and factors by which local communities and their schools can measure progress toward being safe and drug-free

Youth should:

Assume an active role in the development of relevant school policies

Use opportunities for one-on-one contact with at least one adult within the school setting

Participate in community-based opportunities such as community service, local business, local charities, etc.

Families should:

Model responsible use of chemicals, the media, and vehicle safety behaviors

Establish and consistently enforce clear, concise, and appropriate expectations for youth behavior

Encourage the teaching, modeling, and reinforcing of life skills, including refusal skills, conflict resolution skills, deductive reasoning skills, and problem-solving skills

Encourage establishment of local parent resource/ education centers

Communities should:

Establish local coalitions with representatives from all stakeholders to assess community at-risk factors and develop and implement protective strategies for all children and youth

Develop partnerships with schools to increase aspirations for all students

Increase awareness of how schools mirror societal issues and acknowledge local youth violence and drug-usage issues

Encourage law enforcement officials to become involved in youth programs

State Contact

Becky Hayes Boober
> Director of Special Projects
> Maine Department of Education
> 23 State House Station
> Augusta, ME 04333-0023
> (207) 287-5800

Maryland

State Contact

Lou Morrissey, Chief
> Drug-Free Schools Section
> Maryland Department of Education
> 200 West Baltimore Street
> Baltimore, MD 21201
> (410) 767-0301
> (410) 333-2423 (FAX)

Massachusetts

State Contact

John Bynoe
> Education Specialist IV
> Learning Support Services Cluster
> Massachusetts Department of Education
> 350 Main Street
> Malden, MA 02148-5023
> (617) 388-3300, ext. 415
> (617) 388-3476 (FAX)

Michigan

State Contact

Robert E. Peterson, Director
> Drug Education Division
> Office of Drug Control Policy
> P.O. Box 30013
> Lansing, MI 48909
> (517) 373-4700
> (517) 373-2963 (FAX)

Minnesota

Approaches to School Violence Prevention

Minnesota schools are controlled locally with policy set by the school boards. The Department of Children, Families, and Learning provides technical assistance to schools and administers state and federal funding.

The Minnesota legislature appropriates money for violence prevention education in the schools. The money is distributed on a per-pupil-unit basis to districts that have an approved plan for use of their allocation. In addition, the legislature has appropriated money through competitive grants to communities, schools, and nonprofit organizations in a variety of areas dealing with prevention and intervention.

Environmental interventions include identification badges, police liaison officers, and adult building monitors. Some individual schools are considering or have adopted school uniform policies.

Every three years, the Minnesota Department of Children, Families, and Learning conducts a survey of 6th, 9th, and 12th graders on issues related to risk behaviors, resiliency factors, satisfaction, and perception of safety in schools and home life. The *Minnesota Student Survey*, along with the *Weapons Report*, are two main tools used by districts to evaluate their prevention efforts. Many districts have their own internal evaluation tools. Most districts track suspensions, expulsions, referrals to the principal's office, and truancy as measures of the effectiveness of their work, as well as internally produced climate and student satisfaction surveys.

Significant State Legislation

Reports of Dangerous Weapons Incidents in School Zones, State Law 121.207. By 1 February and 1 July of each year, each school zone must report to the commissioner of education incidents involving the use or possession of a dangerous weapon in school zones. The commissioner must compile the information he or she receives from the schools and report it annually to the commissioner of public safety, the criminal and juvenile information policy group, and the legislature.

Expulsion for Possession of Firearm, State Law 127.282. A school board must expel for a period of at least one year a pupil who is determined to have brought a firearm to school. The board may modify this expulsion requirement for a pupil on a case-by-case basis.

School Locker Policy, State Law 127.47. School authorities may inspect the interior of school lockers for any reason at any time, without notice, without student consent, and without a search warrant. A student's personal possessions in a school locker may be searched only when school authorities have a reasonable suspicion that the search will uncover evidence of a violation of law or school rules. As soon as possible after the search of a student's personal possessions, the school authorities must notify the student of the search, unless disclosure would impede an ongoing investigation by police or school officials.

Policy to Refer Firearms Possessor, State Law 127.48. Each school board must have a policy requiring the appropriate school official, as soon as possible, to refer to the criminal justice or juvenile delinquency system, as appropriate, any pupil who brings a firearm to school unlawfully.

State Department of Education Resources

A Bibliography on Violence Prevention

Includes books, papers, topical bibliography, articles, references, resources, and plays.

(For information, contact the Minnesota Department of Children, Families, and Learning, Prevention and Risk Reduction Team.)

Comprehensive Drug and Violence Prevention Application Guidelines

(For information, contact the Minnesota Department of Children, Families, and Learning.)

Dangerous Weapons in Minnesota Schools: State and Federal Laws Pertaining to Reporting and School Policy, 1995–1996

Includes state and federal laws, as well as recommendations for local education systems considering policies that address violence and weapons.

(For information, contact the Minnesota Department of Children, Families, and Learning.)

Dangerous Weapons Incident Report in Minnesota Schools

Reports on weapons incidents at local schools.

(For information on the most recent report, contact the Minnesota Department of Children, Families, and Learning, Office of Community Collaboration, Prevention and Risk Reduction Team.)

Perspectives on Youth: Minnesota Student Survey, 1989, 1992, 1995

Provides a comprehensive picture of Minnesota youth by asking for their perspectives on the positive and negative aspects of their lives and environment. The responses are used by educators, parents, and communities to identify the strengths of young people and respond to their needs and concerns.

(For information, contact the Minnesota Department of Children, Families, and Learning, Office of Community Collaboration.)

Prevention and Intervention Funding for Minnesota's Communities

(For information, call the Application Hotline, 1-800-934-7113.)

Violence Prevention Plan: Unlearning Violence

This statewide plan for violence prevention for schools and communities sets forth seven goals for creating safe, nurturing schools and communities, with challenges and strategies outlined. The plan describes the state education agency's prevention activities, as well as examples of school districts' efforts.

(For information, contact the Minnesota Department of Children, Families, and Learning.)

Violence Prevention Catalogs

A compilation of violence prevention catalogs.

(For information, contact the Minnesota Department of Children, Families, and Learning, Prevention and Risk Reduction Team.)

Violence Prevention Classroom Materials

A compilation of resources drawn from violence prevention curricula, violence and peacemaking literature, staff development material, family resources, and multicultural stories and music.

(For information, contact the Minnesota Department of Children, Families, and Learning, Prevention and Risk Reduction Team.)

Violence Prevention Resource List

A compilation of violence prevention resources.

(For information, contact the Minnesota Department of Children, Families, and Learning, Prevention and Risk Reduction Team.)

Violence Prevention Videos

Lists violence prevention videos reviewed by the Department of Children, Families, and Learning.

(For information, contact the Minnesota Department of Children, Families, and Learning, Prevention and Risk Reduction Team.)

State Contact

Nancy Riestenberg, Violence Prevention Specialist
>   Minnesota Department of Children, Families and Learning
>   550 Cedar Street
>   St. Paul, MN 55101-2273
>   (612) 296-6104
>   (612) 296-3272 (FAX)
>   (612) 297-2094 (TTY)
>   Children@state.mn.us

Mississippi

State Contact

Ginger Steadman, Coordinator
>   Drug-Free Schools Program
>   Department of Education
>   550 High Street
>   Ike Senford Building
>   P.O. Box 771, Suite 205
>   Jackson, MS 39205
>   (601) 359-3915
>   (601) 359-2326 (FAX)

Missouri

Approaches to School Violence Prevention

Each Missouri school district that participates in Title IV of Improving America's Schools Act must have a written violence and drug prevention component in its health curriculum that contains drug and violence prevention objectives for each grade level served by the district. The material must be taught to every student at every grade level annually, including students in preschool programs and in 11th and 12th grades. It must address the legal, social, personal, and health consequences of drug use, promote individual responsibility, and provide information about effective techniques for resisting peer pressure to use drugs.

Funds allocated through this program may be used by local education agencies (LEAs) to develop and implement conflict resolution curricula and programs, character education curricula, and mentoring and/or peer counseling programs. A number of school districts collaborate with local law enforcement agencies to provide officers who come to classrooms and interact with and train students.

The Missouri Department of Education does not endorse any particular resources or programs. Local school districts may select those most closely aligned to their needs. They then send the state Department of Education annual program evaluations that report the extent to which measurable objectives were met for each activity completed under the grant period.

While no technological or environmental interventions have been initiated statewide, limited amounts of a school district's Safe and Drug-Free Schools and Communities Act funds may be spent to establish safe zones of passage between home and school, to acquire and install metal detectors, and to hire security personnel.

Significant State Legislation

The Missouri Department of Education requires all school districts participating in the Safe and Drug-Free Schools and Communities Act of 1994 to comply with the Gun-Free Schools Act of 1994, which requires LEAs to expel from school for a period of not less than one year a student who is determined to have brought a weapon to school.

State Contact

Janet McLelland, Supervisor
  Instructional Improvement and Resources Section
  Department of Elementary and Secondary Education
  P.O. Box 480
  Jefferson City, MO 65102-0480
  (314) 751-6762

Montana

Approaches to School Violence Prevention

No educational, technological, environmental, or regulatory interventions have been mandated at the state level. Approaches to school violence prevention in Montana are being determined at the district level.

State Contact
Spencer Sartorius
    Drug-Free Coordinator
    Department of Education
    Office of Public Instruction
    Capitol Building
    Helena, MT 59620
    (406) 444-4434
    (406) 444-3924 (FAX)

Nebraska

State Contact
Karen Stevens
    Director of Drug-Free Program
    Nebraska Department of Education
    P.O. Box 94987
    301 Centennial Mall South
    Lincoln, NE 68509-4987
    (402) 471-4357
    (402) 471-0117 (FAX)

Nevada

State Contact
Michael Fitzgerald
    Drug Education Consultant
    State Department of Education
    400 West King Street
    Capitol Complex
    Carson City, NV 89710
    (702) 687-3187
    (702) 687-5660 (FAX)

New Hampshire

Approaches to School Violence Prevention
New Hampshire has no formally adopted state program in conflict resolution or peer counseling. However, programs implemented at the district level in 1995 with Safe and Drug-Free Schools and Communities Act grants included:

Student assistance programs to provide counseling to students whose academic progress is impacted by their own or someone else's drug use or violent behavior

Peer mediation programs focused mostly on middle school populations

Conflict resolution skill training for staff and students

Crisis management policies and districtwide discipline policies

Strategies of Limiting Violent Episodes (SOLVE) physical restraint training

Conflict resolution and drug counseling programs

Groups such as New Hampshire Educators for Social Responsibility have worked in many schools across the state. The DARE program is popular with schools and police departments. And the state's Character and Citizenship Program is well known.

With respect to other school violence interventions, some districts in New Hampshire use identification cards and video-cameras on buses.

Significant State Legislation

Safe School Zones, RSA 193D. This law sets forth criminal penalties for any person convicted of an act of theft, destruction, or violence in a safe school zone, including possessing a firearm or other dangerous weapon, at any time of year.

State Department of Education Resources

School Safety Resource Guide

Includes consultants/organizations, school/district programs, alternative programs, and printed material.

State Contact

Gerald P. Bourgeois, Interim Deputy Commissioner
New Hampshire Department of Education
State Office Park South
101 Pleasant Street
Concord, NH 03301
(603) 271-3828
(800) 339-9900 (Citizen Services Line)

New Jersey

Approaches to School Violence Prevention

In the state of New Jersey, kindergarten through 12th grade violence prevention programs developed with funds administered under the Safe Schools Initiative Grant Program for 1996 included:

Infusion of conflict resolution into curricula

Parental involvement in intervention programs

Infusing prejudice reduction into curricula

Creating a parents' advisory board

Staff development in violence prevention, conflict resolution, anger management, and peer mediation

Implementation of counseling services into in-school suspension

Revising student codes of conduct

Implementation of peer mediation programs

Implementation of after-school programs

Developing codes of conduct

Reducing bias incidents through celebration of diversity

Federal Safe and Drug-Free Schools and Communities Act funds have also been dedicated to the establishment of school-located community services centers under the auspices of the New Jersey Department of Human Services.

Finally, New Jersey has a Vandalism, Violence, and Substance Abuse Incident Reporting System, and the Department of Education has funded many violence prevention and intervention initiatives.

Significant State Legislation

Public Safety School Law (1982). This law requires monitoring the incidence of violence in the public schools. Any school employee observing or knowing of a violent act must file a report describing the incident to the school principal and forward a copy to the district superintendent. No employee may be discharged or discriminated against for filing the report.

The principal must notify the superintendent of schools of the action taken regarding the incident. Annually, the superintendent of schools must report to the state Board of Education all acts of violence and vandalism. The Commission of Education must annually submit a report to the Education Committee of the Senate and General Assembly detailing the extent of violence and vandalism in the public schools and make recommendations for alleviating the problem.

Zero Tolerance for Guns Act (1994). Chapter 127 of a 1995 amendment requires that pupils who are convicted or judged delinquent for possession of a firearm or who are found to possess a firearm on school property must be immediately removed from the regular education program and provided with an alternative program, pending a hearing before the Board of Education.

Chapter 128 of a 1995 amendment requires that pupils who commit assaults upon members of the school community with a weapon other than a firearm will also be immediately removed from the regular education program and provided with an alternative program, pending a hearing before the Board of Education.

State Department of Education Resources

Student Codes of Conduct: A Guide to Policy Review and Code Development, fall 1995

Provides a resource for use in developing conduct codes and illustrations of the kinds of approaches districts have found effective.

A Videotape Discussion Guide: Reporting Incidents of Vandalism, Violence, and Substance Abuse, summer 1995

A discussion guide to accompany a videotape on the state's Vandalism, Violence, and Substance Abuse Incident Reporting System. Designed to help school staff regarding their legal responsibility to report incidents of vandalism, violence, and substance abuse. Contains copies of the reporting forms, the definitions, a data table, the Public School Safety Law, and the Zero Tolerance for Guns Act.

A Grant Program to Reduce Student Disruption in Schools: Evaluation Reports/Executive Summary, March 1989

Gives an evaluation of the effectiveness of six alternative education programs under the two-year Grant Program to Reduce Student Disruption in Schools.

The New Jersey Department of Education Violence and Vandalism Prevention Task Force, 5 January 1994

Recommendations of a task force created in 1993, composed of parents, students, teachers, administrators, state agency and educational association representatives, and law enforcement officials, that was charged with addressing issues of school violence. Recommendations are made in the areas of community and parent/guardian involvement, policy, professional development, organization and structure, instructional issues, programs, state reporting, and support.

Safe Schools Initiative: Creating a Safe, Disciplined School Environment Conducive to Learning, July 1994

Gives an overview of school violence issues, the Department of Education's past and current efforts in prevention and intervention, state board regulations related to school violence, and the Department of Education's violence and vandalism prevention task force recommendations.

Violence, Vandalism, and Substance Abuse in New Jersey Schools 1991–1992: The Commissioner's Report to the Education Committees of the Senate and General Assembly, March 1993

Analyzes the county summaries of incidents of violence at the school level from the school year 1991–1992.

The State Memorandum of Agreement between Education and Law Enforcement Officials, April 1992

Text of the agreement between the New Jersey Department of Education and the New Jersey Department of Law and Public Safety for use by local law enforcement and education officials. Documents the commitment by both professional communities to work together to address the state's drug problem as it relates to school-aged children.

A Guide for the Operation and Approval of Alternative Schools/ Programs, spring 1992

Sets forth the requirements for the operation of alternative high schools and programs for students who are not succeeding in their present school settings and who require increasing amounts of professional time and attention from school staff.

Developing Character and Values in New Jersey Students: A Manual of Promising Programs and Practices, July 1992 (Bureau of Student Support Services)

Provides educators in New Jersey public schools with a resource manual of promising character and values education programs implemented in other states and school districts. Programs were not judged against state criteria of effectiveness but represent a description of what is currently in place.

A Survey of District Activity in Character and Values Education, November 1992 (Bureau of Student Support Services, Division of Educational Programs and Student Services)

Includes results assessment of the level and types of district activity in character and values education.

State Contact

Philip M. Brown, Ph.D.
>   Coordinator of Programs and Policy
>   Office of Safe and Drug-Free Schools
>   New Jersey Department of Education
>   CN500
>   Trenton, NJ 08625-0500
>   (609) 292-4461

New Mexico

Approaches to School Violence Prevention

Within the last two years, New Mexico has received a grant to fund its character education program called Character Count. Also, its mediation program, which has been in operation for several years, has received much national notoriety.

State Contact

Nancy Mandel
>   State Supervisor for School Counseling
>   New Mexico Department of Education
>   300 Don Gaspar
>   Santa Fe, NM 87501-2786
>   (505) 827-6698

New York

Approaches to School Violence Prevention

Each school district in the state of New York uses the educational approaches and technological/environmental and regulatory interventions that meet its needs, using funding from grants provided under the Safe and Drug-Free Schools and Communities Act of 1994. The state Education Department, however, does not request that each district address all types of approaches and interventions in order to receive funding.

Each school district undertakes its own evaluation of programs related to school violence. The state Education Department has not undertaken any statewide evaluation of such programs.

State Contact

Arlene Sheffield
    Education Department
    The University of the State of New York
    Comprehensive Health and Pupil Services
    Room 318M EB
    Albany, NY 12234
    (518) 486-6090
    (518) 486-7290 (FAX)

North Carolina

State Contact

Olivia Oxendine
    Chief Consultant for Student Support Services
    301 North Wilmington Street
    Raleigh, NC 27603-1725
    (919) 715-1735
    (919) 715-1897 (FAX)

North Dakota

State Contact

David L. Lee, Director
    Department of Public Instruction
    Office of Chemical Health
    State Capitol, 9th Floor
    Bismark, ND 58505
    (701) 328-2254
    (701) 328-4770 (FAX)

Ohio

State Contact

Judy Airhart, Assistant Director
    Student Development Division
    Ohio Department of Education
    65 South Front Street, Room 719
    Columbus, OH 43215-4183
    (614) 466-2471
    (614) 728-3768 (FAX)

Oklahoma

State Contact

Dan Reich
    Director of Comprehensive Health
    State Department of Education
    2500 North Lincoln Boulevard
    Oklahoma City, OK 73105-4599
    (405) 521-4507
    (405) 521-6205 (FAX)

Oregon

State Contact

Judy Miller
    Assistant Superintendent
    Oregon Department of Education
    255 Capitol Street, NE
    Salem, OR 97310
    (503) 378-5585
    (503) 378-7968 (FAX)

Pennsylvania

Approaches to School Violence Prevention

The state of Pennsylvania has developed a Center for Safe
Schools that provides schools with technical assistance and
training in such areas as peer mediation, developing school
safety plans, and the effects of domestic violence.

Significant State Legislation

Act 26 of 1995. This legislation implements the federal Gun-Free legislative mandate; requires the state Department of Education to set up an Office of Safe Schools; requires the Office of Safe Schools to conduct statewide data collection on the scope of the violence problem in the schools; and sets record-keeping standards for the maintenance, retention, and transfer of students' disciplinary records.

State Contact

Sandra J. Rakar, Program Coordinator
  Network for Student Assistance Services
  Pennsylvania Department of Education
  333 Market Street
  Harrisburg, PA 17126-0333
  (717) 783-6788

Rhode Island

State Contact

George McDonough, Coordinator
  Drug-Free Schools and Communities Act Program
  Rhode Island Department of Education
  22 Hayes Street, Room 313
  Providence, RI 02908
  (401) 277-6523
  (401) 277-4979 (FAX)

South Carolina

Approaches to School Violence Prevention

South Carolina uses conflict resolution curricula, such as "Second Step, K–8," for skills in building empathy, anger management, impulse control, and problem solving. The state has provided training to 34 individuals at the district level in implementing this curriculum. Other curricula in use include "Peace Works" and "Working toward Peace." Also, mentoring and peer mediation programs are widespread in this state.

State education superintendent Barbara S. Nielsen, working in concert with religious, legislative, and community leaders, has built a strong character education initiative in South Carolina. Nielsen has sought input from all communities in the state on what they see as the necessary building blocks of character and what should be reinforced in local schools.

Alternative schools are gaining popularity. They offer a highly structured environment for students who have been expelled or whose disruptive behavior in regular classrooms has placed them in danger of expulsion. Eligible students wear uniforms, maintain military haircuts, and are inspected for personal hygiene. There are 17 days of military-style boot camp training, followed by a rigid schedule of academic training, a physical training regimen, and on- and off-site work projects and community service.

There are several notable model programs in this state. In the Columbia High School Mentoring Program (CAPS), for example, each faculty member, including the principal, is assigned 13–15 students across grade levels to mentor twice a month in areas such as academics, personal problems, conflict resolution, career direction, and being a trusted adult friend to the students.

The Sumter school district has a program requiring expelled students to complete a 15-hour course in behavior management. It offers staff development in "Managing Aggressive and Hostile Students." It also conducts a "Turn Off the Violence" campaign.

In Richland 2 Alternative School, local physicians volunteer to meet with students and describe some of the tragedies they see in emergency rooms, such as teens who have been shot, assault victims, drug- or alcohol-related accident victims, etc.

Thirty-three schools in the Charleston school district have decided to incorporate school uniforms into their strategy for better discipline and safety. Technological prevention strategies include surveillance cameras on school buses and in schools, metal detectors in schools, ID badges for students and staff, and inclusion of safety elements in the suggestions for facilities planning.

School Resource Office programs are gaining popularity in South Carolina. Federal funds are matched 75–25 by school districts wishing to employ a school resource officer, a uniformed presence on the school campus who provides help and information to students and staff.

South Carolina mandates comprehensive data collection on all school criminal incidents committed on school grounds, on buses or other school transportation, and at school functions. The annual report helps target resources to the greatest needs.

Significant State Legislation

The state's Gun-Free Schools Law, pursuant to federal law requirements, requires that students determined to have brought guns to school be expelled for one year, although the local superintendent can modify the expulsion on a case-by-case basis.

Other laws in this state:

Allow principals to conduct reasonable searches, with or without cause, of anyone and anything on school grounds (no strip searches are allowed, however)

Require school administrators to report immediately to law enforcement any injury or serious threat of injury to persons or property on school grounds

Require law enforcement to notify school administrators when an enrolled student is taken into custody for any violation other than a wildlife or traffic violation

State Contact

Bunny Mack
Education Program Associate
Safe and Drug-Free Schools
South Carolina Department of Education
1429 Senate Street
Columbia, SC 29201
(803) 734-8566/8573
(803) 734-7896 (FAX)

South Dakota

Approaches to School Violence Prevention

Unlike most states grappling with violence-related incidents and issues, South Dakota is experiencing relatively few problems related to violence and drug use by school-aged children. Nevertheless, the state has taken such preventive measures as using the DARE program, mentoring, peer counseling, conflict resolution, character education, and teacher training in school violence prevention.

At the present time, no evaluation has been done on any of the state's efforts at school violence prevention.

State Department of Education Resources
South Dakota Youth Risk Behavior Survey Report, 1995

Reports the results of South Dakota's 1995 Youth Risk Behavior Survey. Administered biennially, this questionnaire consists of 95 items that assess the six priority health risk behaviors that result in the greatest amount of morbidity, mortality, and social problems among youth: intentional and unintentional injuries; tobacco use; alcohol and other drug use; sexual behaviors that result in HIV infection, other sexually transmitted diseases, and unintended pregnancy; dietary behaviors; and physical activity.

State Contact
Don Schanadore, Drug-Free Coordinator
>Department of Education and Cultural Affairs
>700 Governors Drive
>Pierre, SD 57501-2291
>(605) 773-4670
>(605) 773-6139 (FAX)

Tennessee
State Contact
Mike Hermann
>Coordinator for Drug-Free School Program
>Department of Education, 6F1
>Gateway Plaza
>710 James Robertson Parkway
>Nashville, TN 37243-0375
>(615) 741-3248
>(615) 741-6236 (FAX)

Texas
State Contact
B. J. Gibson
>Director of Programs & State Coordinator
>   for Drug-Free Schools and Communities
>Division of Accelerated Instruction
>1701 North Congress Avenue
>Austin, TX 78701-1494
>(512) 463-9006
>(512) 475-2619 (FAX)

Utah

State Contact
Verne Larsen
Education Program Specialist
Utah Office of Education
Drug-Free Schools Program
250 East 500 South
Salt Lake City, UT 84111
(801) 538-7713
(801) 538-7521 (FAX)

Vermont

State Contact
Susan Mahoney, Coordinator
Drug-Free Schools Program
Vermont Department of Education
120 State Street
Montpelier, VT 05620-2703
(802) 828-3124
(802) 828-3140 (FAX)

Virginia

Approaches to School Violence Prevention
The Virginia Department of Education has provided training to state educators in implementing conflict resolution and/or peer mediation programs. According to a recent survey, some 50 percent of school divisions currently include conflict mediation in their programs. Although the Department of Education has no data to indicate the number of character education programs or curricula currently being used, the state recently applied for a federal grant to fund the development of character education curricula.

Most school divisions in Virginia have developed partnerships with local law enforcement agencies, though the state does not collect data to indicate how many or to what extent. Law enforcement may provide such services as conducting site assessments, providing school resource officers, or providing DARE officers.

In Virginia, school safety is primarily a local district issue. Thus, the districts differ in their policy and use of such technology as metal scanners, retrofitting, and resource materials. The Department of Education offers technical assistance as requested that may include staff development, resource materials, consulting, etc. In addition, the state collects annual data on incidents of crime, violence, and substance abuse.

Significant State Legislation

In 1994, the Virginia legislature passed its version of the federal Gun-Free Schools Act of 1994.

State Contact

Marsha O. Hubbard, School Safety Specialist
    Virginia Department of Education
    P.O. Box 2120
    Richmond, VA 23216-2120
    (804) 225-2928

Washington

State Contact

Denise L. Fitch, Acting Supervisor
    Substance Abuse Education
    Drug-Free Schools and Communities Program
    Office of the Superintendent of Public Instruction
    Old Capitol Building
    P.O. Box 47200
    Olympia, WA 98504-7200
    (360) 753-5595
    (360) 664-3028 (FAX)

West Virginia

Approaches to School Violence Prevention

Conflict resolution/peer mediation programs are among the educational approaches the state of West Virginia uses to prevent school violence. In 1994 the state legislature mandated that conflict resolution skills be taught in West Virginia schools.

The Responsible Students Program was developed at Wheeling Middle School as the Program for Internalizing Values Obtained through School (PIVOTS) to encourage responsible student behavior. West Virginia Governor Gaston Caperton, during the 1992–1993 school year, requested the state Board of Education to expand the program to all West Virginia public schools. The program helps students become organized, dependable, and accountable individuals capable of making good judgments. Evidence suggests that the Responsible Students Program has improved school performance by 33 percent, as well as attendance, school citizenship, and active participation in class. Schools that have implemented the program report that it has resulted in the avoidance of conflict and contributes to a safe environment.

Like Florida, West Virginia offers Student Assistance Programs (SAPs) that identify and offer assistance to students troubled by physical, emotional, social, legal, educational, sexual, medical, family, or chemical-based problems. SAPs focus on prevention intervention and aftercare services for students returning from treatment.

In addition, as the result of nine Safe School summits held throughout the state between January and April 1994 in which students, educators, and community leaders discussed violence prevention, individual schools developed their own action plans to address top concerns.

Significant State Legislation

Senate Bill 46. This legislation prohibits the possession of a deadly weapon on a school bus, in any public or private school or secondary vocational school or on their grounds, in premises that house courts of law, and in the offices of family law masters. The bill also requires school principals to report weapons violations that occur on buses or at school buildings and grounds to the state Board of Education and to the local state police.

Senate Bill 1000. This bill mandates the teaching of resistance and life skills within existing health and physical education classes to counteract societal pressure to use drugs, alcohol, and tobacco. It also mandates prescribed programs to coordinate violence reduction efforts in schools and calls for the state Board of Education to prescribe programs to coordinate violence reduction efforts in schools and between schools and communities. Finally, it states that students, teachers, counselors, and staff shall be trained in conflict resolution skills.

State Department of Education Resources

Profile of the Safe Schools Initiative: Summits, Issues, Solutions, Actions, Programs, Legislation

Reports the concerns and solutions generated by students during the nine Safe School summits sponsored by the West

Virginia Department of Education from January to April 1994. Provides information that can be used to formulate activities and programs that support a safe school environment.

State Contact
Therese M. Wilson, Director
      Office of Student Services and Assessment
      West Virginia Department of Education
      Capitol Building #6
      Room B-057
      1900 Kanawha Boulevard East
      Charleston, WV 245305
      (304) 558-2546

Wisconsin

Approaches to School Violence Prevention

For several years, schools in Wisconsin have used multi-strategy prevention approaches that deal with one or more youth risk behaviors. The state's Student Services/Prevention and Wellness Team at the Department of Public Instruction has designed a Framework for Student Services, Prevention, and Wellness to build on and enhance the strengths of Wisconsin schools' current programs. The Framework is organized into six components: Healthy School Environment; Curriculum, Instruction, and Assessment; Pupil Services; Student Programs; Adult Programs; and Family and Community Connections.

The purposes of the Framework are (1) to communicate the role schools play in the positive development of healthy, resilient, successful learners; (2) to help schools create an integrated service delivery system; and (3) to act as a functional system for the Student Services/Prevention and Wellness Team for integrating the services, programs, and funds related to prevention and the health and development of children.

Schools may adapt or adopt the Framework. Schools and communities are free to design their own strategies that address youth risk behaviors and promote health and youth development.

State Department of Education Resources
Framework for an Integrated Approach to Student Services, Prevention, and Wellness Programs

Outlines the state's Student Services/Prevention and Wellness Team approach in addressing youth risk behaviors and promoting the health, well-being, and positive development of students and other members of the school community.

Self-Assessment Tool for Integrated and Comprehensive Student Services, Prevention, and Wellness Programs

A self-assessment instrument intended for schools or school districts to determine how they have progressed toward integration of their Student Services, Prevention, and Wellness programs.

State Contact

Michael J. Thompson, Team Leader
    Student Services/Prevention and Wellness Team
    Wisconsin Department of Public Instruction
    P.O. Box 7841
    Madison, WI 53707-7841
    (608) 266-3390
    (608) 267-2427 (TDD)

Wyoming

Approaches to School Violence Prevention

The 49 school districts of Wyoming are responsible for the activities that take place within their jurisdiction. Thus, there are many different approaches to violence prevention being used in this state. The state Department of Education does not collect information on the methods used, so there is no evaluation on a state level of the techniques that work. At this time, no districts are using any technological or environmental interventions.

Significant State Legislation

Wyoming has a weapon-free school zone law to combat the problem of weapons in schools. Many school districts have adopted a zero tolerance for weapons on students.

State Contact

D. Leeds Pickering
    Wyoming Department of Education
    Hathaway Building, Second Floor
    2300 Capitol Avenue
    Cheyenne, WY 82002-0050
    (307) 777-6265

Organizations, Conferences, and Training

Organizations

Whether you are a researcher, a violence prevention practitioner, a policymaker, an educator, or a concerned citizen, this directory will guide you to key resources in school violence prevention. Since the field is ever-expanding, this list is by no means exhaustive. These organizations, however, have established reputations and will prove a good starting point for an information search.

If you are exploring the causes and prevention of violence, three organizations provide up-to-date research: (1) the Center for the Study and Prevention of Violence, (2) the Centers for Disease Control and Prevention, and (3) the National Center for Injury Prevention and Control. For current juvenile crime statistics, contact the Juvenile Justice Clearinghouse, the National Center for Juvenile Justice, and the National Criminal Justice Reference Service.

To network with violence prevention practitioners, contact the National Network of Violence Prevention Practitioners at the Education Development Center (EDC). Annual conferences and training programs provide excellent networking opportunities.

If you are searching for educational

resources such as violence prevention and conflict resolution curricula, get in touch with the Center for the Study and Prevention of Violence, the EDC, the National Association for Mediation in Education, the National Institute for Dispute Resolution, and the National School Safety Center. Professional educators should also contact the American Federation of Teachers, Educators for Social Responsibility, the National Association of Secondary School Principals, the National Association of State Boards of Education, the National Education Association of the United States, and the National School Boards Association.

The U.S. Department of Education provides information on the Safe and Drug-Free Schools program, the National Education Goals, and school violence prevention legislation.

If you want to establish a crime prevention program in your community, contact the Harvard School of Public Health and the President's Crime Prevention Council.

The remainder of the resources listed in this directory will help you explore such specific areas as character education, the needs of at-risk and urban youth, crisis intervention and public risk management, children's radio and television programming, drug and alcohol information, gun safety, and school security.

American Federation of Teachers (AFT)
555 New Jersey Avenue, NW
Washington, DC 20001
(202) 879-4400

The AFT represents 900,000 teachers, paraprofessionals, school-related personnel, public and municipal employees, higher education faculty and staff, and nurses and other health professionals. It advocates national standards for education, the professionalization of teaching, and disciplined and safe environments for learning.

The AFT has actively promoted safe schools practices over the years. One recent initiative is its "Zero Tolerance" policy for drugs, weapons, violence, and disruptive behavior in and around schools. The AFT is currently waging a national campaign called "Responsibility, Respect, Results: Lessons for Life." It has a strong antiviolence component and promotes higher academic and discipline standards.

American Psychological Association (APA)
750 First Street, NE
Washington, DC 20002-4242

(202) 336-5500
(202) 336-6123 (FAX)

The APA is the major organization representing psychology in the United States and the world's largest association of psychologists. Since its founding in 1892, it has worked toward the advancement of psychology as a science, a profession, and a means of promoting human welfare.

Publications: Offers publication on youth violence, including "Raising Children to Resist Violence: What You Can Do" (pamphlet produced collaboratively with the American Academy of Pediatrics), "Violence and Youth" (booklet), and *Reason to Hope: A Psychosocial Perspective on Violence and Youth* (text).

American School Health Association (ASHA)
7263 State Route 43
P.O. Box 708
Kent, OH 44240
(330) 678-1601
(330) 678-4526 (FAX)
Diane D. Allensworth, Executive Director

The American School Health Association (ASHA) unites more than 3,000 professionals in 56 countries who are working in schools and are committed to safeguarding the health of school-aged children, preschool through grade 12, and of the professionals who serve them. The ASHA is a multidisciplinary organization of administrators, counselors, dentists, health educators, physical educators, school nurses, and school physicians. It advocates high-quality school health instruction, health services, and a healthy school environment. Benefits of membership include information on safety and violence prevention resources. The ASHA's Council on Unintentional Injury and Violence Prevention is chaired by Susan Gallagher at the Education Development Center, 55 Chapel Street, Newton, MA 02158-1060, (617) 244-3436.

The Center for the Study and Prevention of Violence (CSPV)
Institute of Behavioral Science
University of Colorado at Boulder
Campus Box 442
Boulder, CO 80309-0442
(303) 492-8465
(303) 443-3297 (FAX)

cspv@colorado.edu
http://www.colorado.edu/cspv
For information, ask for an Information House Specialist.

A nonprofit research and information organization committed to building bridges between the research community, the practitioner community, and policymakers working to understand and prevent violence, particularly adolescent violence. Accomplishes its mission in three ways. First, an Information House collects research literature on the causes and prevention of violence and provides direct information services to the public by offering topical bibliographic searches. Second, the CSPV offers evaluation technical assistance to violence prevention programs. Third, it maintains a basic research component through data analysis and other projects on the causes of violence and the effectiveness of prevention and intervention programs. (See databases in chapter 7.)

Center to Prevent Handgun Violence
1225 Eye Street, NW
Suite 1100
Washington, DC 20005
(202) 289-7319
(202) 682-4462 (FAX)
Nancy P. Gannon, Director of Education Division

A national education, legal action, and research organization founded in 1983 to educate U.S. citizens about the scope of gun violence and to prevent further bloodshed. Offers curriculum called STAR (Straight Talk about Risks) used in 32 districts, including New York, Los Angeles, Chicago, and Dade County, Florida.

Centers for Disease Control and Prevention (CDC)
4770 Buford Highway, NE
Atlanta, GA 30341
(404) 639-3311
(404) 488-4677 (Automated Injury Information Line)

The CDC is the lead federal agency for public health in this country. It takes a public health approach to solving youth violence because of its impact on the health and well-being of our youth and works to identify patterns and risk factors, implement interventions, and evaluate their effectiveness.

Beginning in fiscal year 1992, the CDC funded 12 one- to three-year cooperative agreements to evaluate specific interventions that may reduce injuries and deaths related to interpersonal violence among adolescents and young adults. In fiscal year 1993, the CDC funded three five-year cooperative agreements to evaluate more comprehensive programs with multiple interventions. (See National Center for Injury Prevention and Control.)

Character Education Partnership (CEP)
809 Franklin Street
Alexandria, VA 22314-4105
(800) 988-8081
(703) 739-9515
(703) 739-4967 (FAX)
geninfo@character.org
http://web2010.com/cepweb
A. John Martin, Executive Director

The CEP is the national advocacy group for character education. It operates a resource center for character education information and disseminates key publications and resource lists that can assist teachers, parents, school board members, and school administrators in their efforts to plan and implement character-developing activities. The CEP's annual Character Education Forum brings together the thought leaders and practitioners in the field. In addition to its individual members and many character education and ethics centers and institutes, the CEP counts the American Association of School Administrators, the American Federation of Teachers, the Association for Supervision and Curriculum Development, the National Association of Secondary School Principals, the National Council for Social Studies, the National Education Association, and the National School Boards Association among its 70 organizational members.

Child Development Project (CDP)
Developmental Studies Center
2000 Embarcadero
Suite 305
Oakland, CA 94606
(510) 533-0213
(510) 464-3670 (FAX)
Eric Schaps, Program Director

The CDP is a demonstration project designed to enhance the ethical, social, and intellectual development of children through systematic changes in the classroom, school, and home environment.

Children's Defense Fund (CDF)
25 E Street, NW
Washington, DC 20001
(202) 628-8787
(202) 662-3530 (FAX)

The CDF exists to provide a voice for children in the United States, paying particular attention to the needs of poor, minority, and disabled children. Its goal is to educate the nation about the needs of children and encourage preventive investment in children before they get sick, drop out of school, suffer family breakdown, or get into trouble.

The CDF focuses on programs and policies that affect large numbers of children. It gathers data and disseminates information on key issues affecting children and monitors the development and implementation of federal and state policies. It provides information, technical assistance, and support to a network of state and local child advocates, service providers, and public and private sector officials and leaders.

The CDF pursues an annual legislative agenda in Congress and in states where it has offices. It also educates thousands of citizens annually about children's needs and responsible options for meeting them. The Black Community Crusade for Children, coordinated by the CDF, is an initiative to mobilize the African-American community behind a targeted effort to address the special problems facing black children.

Committee for Children
2203 Airport Way South
Suite 500
Seattle, WA 98134-2027
(800) 634-4449
(206) 343-1223
(206) 343-1445 (FAX)

The Committee for Children is an independent nonprofit organization that has researched and developed social skills curricula since the late 1970s and offers prekindergarten through grade eight violence prevention school curricula, as well as training for educators. Its mission is to promote the safety, well-being, and social development of children by creating quality educational programs for educators, families, and communities. Chief among its violence prevention curricula is "Second Step," which is now used nationwide in teaching children to change the attitudes and behaviors that contribute to violence.

Council of the Great City Schools
1301 Pennsylvania Avenue, NW
Suite 702
Washington, DC 20004
(202) 393-2427
Henry Duvall, Director of Communications

The only organization in the nation exclusively representing the needs of urban public schools, the Council of the Great City Schools is composed of 48 large city school districts. It promotes the cause of urban schools and acts as an advocate for inner-city students through legislation, research, and media relations. Reports on the initiatives of various school districts to combat school violence. It also provides a network for school districts sharing common problems to exchange information and collectively address new challenges in order to deliver the best education for the nation's urban youth.

Publications: Offers publications on such issues as urban school safety, AIDS education and HIV prevention programs in urban schools, and minority student access to and preparation for higher education. Also offers a video entitled *Town Hall Meeting on School Safety and Violence.*

Education Development Center (EDC)
55 Chapel Street
Newton, MA 02158
(617) 969-7100
(617) 244-3436 (FAX)
http://www.edc.org/home.html
Rebecca Atnafou, Associate Project Director

The EDC is a nonprofit organization that has worked in injury prevention and control since 1975 and in violence prevention since 1986. Its goal is to make a major contribution to the reduction of violence across the life cycle. To that end, it develops and evaluates middle school through grade 12 violence prevention curricula. "The Violence Prevention Curriculum for Adolescents" is currently used nationwide in more than 5,000 programs, including schools, hospitals, and community agencies.

The EDC operates the Adolescent Violence Prevention Resource Center (AVPRC—one of six such centers that compose the Children's Safety Network, a national resource for child and adolescent injury and prevention funded by the Maternal and Child Health Bureau of the U.S. Department of Health and Human Services). The AVPRC offers databases of information, develops violence prevention curricula and other materials, and plans and conducts site visits.

Also operated by the EDC is the National Network of Violence Prevention Practitioners (NNVPP) , a network of members dedicated to preventing violence among our nation's youth. Anyone active in the field of adolescent violence prevention— including violence prevention programs, schools, community-based and national organizations, university faculty, criminal justice, and public health agencies—is eligible for membership. Benefits include a quarterly bulletin, fact sheets, access to the NNVPP World Wide Web homepage, reproducible violence prevention material, and a membership directory.

For more information on the National Network of Violence Prevention Practitioners, contact Christopher Hass, (617) 969-7100, ext. 2380, or the NNVPP homepage web site at http://www.edc.org/HHD/NNVPP.

Educators for Social Responsibility (ESR)
23 Garden Street
Cambridge, MA 02138
(800) 370-2515
(617) 492-1764
(617) 864-5164 (FAX)
http://www.benjerry.com/esr

The ESR provides resources and services for educators and parents, including books; curricula; and workshops and training on violence prevention, conflict resolution, intergroup relations, and character education. Query the web site for information on the highly regarded Resolving Conflict Creatively Program and other materials.

Harvard School of Public Health
Office of Government and Community Programs
Program for Health Care Negotiation and Conflict Resolution
Violence Prevention Programs
718 Huntington Avenue

1st Floor
Boston, MA 02115
(617) 432-0814
(617) 432-0068 (FAX)

Sher Quaday, Director, Violence Prevention Programs

The Community Violence Prevention Project (CVPP) at the Harvard School of Public Health was formed to develop a how-to manual *(Peace by Piece: A Guide for Preventing Community Violence)* that will help citizens establish antiviolence programs in their communities. It also serves as a resource center for information gathering and dissemination and as a national evaluation center to provide assistance and information to program operators, grantmakers, policymakers, community leaders, and educators.

Juvenile Justice Clearinghouse (JJC)
Office of Juvenile Justice and Delinquency Prevention (OJJDP)
A Component of the National Criminal Justice
    Reference Service (NCJRS)
P.O. Box 6000
Rockville, MD 20849-6000
(800) 638-8736
(301) 738-8895 (Direct Dial through modem to the
    NCJRS Electronic Bulletin Board)
http://www.look@ncjrs.aspensys.com (to receive outline
of services of NCJRS)

The JJC is a service of the Office of Juvenile Justice and Delinquency Prevention (OJJDP), which is a component of the National Criminal Justice Reference Service (NCJRS). It links the OJJDP with juvenile justice practitioners, policymakers, and the public; maintains a toll-free number for information requests and prepares specialized responses to those requests; collects, synthesizes, and disseminates information on all areas of juvenile justice; and distributes OJJDP publications covering juvenile justice.

Publications: The JJC provides a free copy of *Juvenile Offenders and Victims: A National Report* (August 1995). The NCJRS Bulletin Board System provides much information and publications from the five Office of Justice Programs agencies (the National Institute of Justice, the Office of Juvenile Justice and Delinquency Prevention, the Office for Victims of Crime, the Bureau of Justice Statistics, and the Bureau of Justice Assistance) and the Office for National Drug Control Policy.

KIDSNET
6856 Eastern Avenue, NW
Suite 208
Washington, DC 20012
kidsnet@aol.com

KIDSNET is a computerized clearinghouse for children's television and radio.

Publications: Offers a free guide to publications and groups concerned about violence.

Metropolitan Life Insurance Company
P.O. Box 807
Madison Square Station
New York, NY 10159-0807

The Metropolitan Life Insurance Company conducts an annual "Metropolitan Life Survey of the American Teacher," which explores teachers' opinions and brings them to the attention of the U.S. public and policymakers. The 1993 survey was called "Violence in America's Public Schools."

National Association for Mediation in Education (NAME)
c/o National Institute for Dispute Resolution (NIDR)
1726 M Street, NW
Suite 500
Washington, DC 20036-4502
(202) 466-4764
(202) 466-4769 (FAX)
nidr@igc.apc.org

Part of the nonprofit National Institute for Dispute Resolution (NIDR), the NAME promotes the development, implementation, and institutionalization of school- and university-based conflict resolution programs and curricula. It currently serves as the primary national and international clearinghouse for information, resources, technical assistance, and training in the field of conflict resolution in education. It also provides models for conflict resolution, publications, an annual conference, networking opportunities, technical assistance with new and existing programs, and research. Individual and organizational memberships are available.

Publications: Provides a catalog of conflict resolution education materials and a newsletter, the *Fourth R.*

National Association of Secondary School Principals (NASSP)
1904 Association Drive
Reston, VA 22091-1537
(703) 860-0200
(703) 476-5432 (FAX)

Timothy J. Dyer, Executive Director

Established in 1916, the NASSP has more than 41,000 members and is the nation's largest school leadership organization for middle and high school administrators. It provides a wide range of programs, services, and publications; promotes the interests of school administrators in Congress; provides consulting services on such topics as instructional improvement, student government, and urban education; and sponsors student- oriented programs such as the National Association of Student Councils, the National Honor Society, and Partnerships International.

Publications: Offers *Safe Schools: A Handbook for Practitioners*, a reference for school leaders that provides step-by-step instruction focusing on school security and implementing preventive measures.

National Association of State Boards of Education (NASBE)
1012 Cameron Street
Alexandria, VA 22314
(703) 684-4000
(703) 836-2313 (FAX)
boards@nasbe.org

Thomas Davis, President Elect

The NASBE is a nonprofit, private association that represents state and territorial boards of education. Its mission is to strengthen state boards of education by serving and representing them in their effort to ensure quality education. In 1994, the NASBE conducted a study group on violence and its impact on schools and learning. Countering policy trends that rely solely on the blanket expulsion of students caught with weapons, the NASBE's resulting report, *Schools without Fear*, has called for addressing the U.S. youth violence epidemic on multiple fronts, "using a creative balance of preventive as well as punitive strategies that target the individual, the home, the school, and the community." For more information, contact Carlos Vega-Matos, Project Director.

National Center for Injury Prevention and Control (NCIPC)
Division of Violence Prevention
Centers for Disease Control and Prevention (CDC)
4770 Buford Highway, NE
Atlanta, GA 30333
(404) 639-3311

Growing recognition of the public health importance of injuries led to the formation in July 1992 of the National Center for Injury Prevention and Control (NCIPC) at the Centers for Disease Control and Prevention (CDC), within which the Division of Violence Prevention was established in October 1993. Today, more than 30 CDC researchers and program managers study violence using the same kinds of public health tools applied to infectious diseases, chronic diseases, and occupational hazards. All of the NCIPC research efforts somehow touch on the problem of youth violence. For example, complementing the efforts of the Department of Justice, NCIPC researches what prevents youth from becoming victims or perpetrators of violence. It is currently evaluating 15 projects across the country that represent a broad range of interventions for children and adolescents at various stages of development.

The NCIPC sponsors research that examines what puts young people at risk for violence. It is cosponsoring several large projects to implement violence prevention strategies in specific settings. In addition, it advises communities on promising strategies by distributing a manual entitled *The Prevention of Youth Violence: A Framework for Community Action.*

The NCIPC raises awareness of suicide as a serious public health problem, especially with the young, and of effective prevention strategies. It has published a surveillance report, *Suicide in the United States, 1980–1992,* which outlines rates of suicide in this country and trends over time. Activities in this area include the development of methods to screen and identify youth at risk of suicide, monitoring suicidal behavior of adolescents through the CDC's Youth Risk Behavior Surveillance System, and making information available to communities interested in carrying out prevention programs through the publication of *Youth Suicide Prevention Programs: A Resource Guide.*

Finally, the NCIPC sponsors several projects that will help characterize the problem of family and intimate violence in the United States. A representative project will study the factors that affect the psychological health and well-being of children who witness intimate violence by a man against a woman. The researchers will measure children's exposure to violence (both as a witness and as a victim), injuries from abuse, experiences of internalizing and externalizing behavior problems such as depression and aggression, social supports, family stressors, and school achievement over the first nine months following their stay in a domestic violence shelter. The NCIPC is seeking to know more about how effective specific interventions are and how to combine them into programs that can be placed in communities, workplaces, schools, and other settings. (See Centers for Disease Control and Prevention.)

Publications: The NCIPC has published several works on the topic of violence prevention, such as those mentioned above.

National Center for Juvenile Justice (NCJJ)
710 Fifth Avenue, 3rd Floor
Pittsburgh, PA 15219-3000
(412) 227-6950
(412) 227-6955 (FAX)

The NCJJ offers information on policies/regulations/laws, statistics and research, training/technical assistance, publications, and program evaluation.

National Clearinghouse on Alcohol and Other Drug Information (NCADI)
P.O. Box 2345
Rockville, MD 20852
(800) 729-6686
(301) 468-6433

The NCADI is the primary federal clearinghouse supplying information about alcohol and drug use prevention and treatment topics. Another toll-free number, (800) 788-2900, accesses all federally sponsored clearinghouses that provide information concerning drug issues.

National Criminal Justice Reference Service (NCJRS)
P.O. Box 6000
Rockville, MD 20849
(800) 851-3420
(301) 251-5212 (FAX)

The NCJRS serves as a single point of contact for the National Institute of Justice, the Office of Juvenile Justice and Delinquency Prevention, the Office for Victims of Crime, the Bureau of Justice

Statistics, the Bureau of Justice Assistance, and the Office of National Drug Control Policy.

National Crisis Prevention Institute (CPI)
3315-K North 124th Street
Brookfield, WI 53005
(800) 558-8976
(414) 783-5787
(414) 783-5906 (FAX)
cpi@execpc.com
http://www.execpc.com/-cpi

Linda Steiger, Director. For more information, ask for a Training Support Specialist.

The CPI has been training human service professionals in how to manage disruptive and assaultive behavior safely since 1980. The CPI's Nonviolence Crisis Intervention Program is the most widely used method in the United States for defusing confrontations and is used by thousands of schools and youth service agencies throughout the United States and Canada. It offers various training options, including a one-day seminar, a two-day workshop, and a four-day intensive Instructor Certification Program. Training programs are scheduled at various locations and dates across the country. It also offers customized Inservice Training options, video training programs such as "The Assaultive Student," "Fights at School," and "Effective Documentation of School Incidents," and related services. Call for references from educators in a facility near you who are currently using the CPI's Nonviolent Crisis Intervention Program.

National Education Association of the United States (NEA)
1201 16th Street, NW
Washington, DC 20036-3290
(202) 833-4000
http://www.nea.org

Bob Chase, President

The NEA is the nation's largest professional association and employee organization. Its purposes are to promote the cause of quality public education and advance the profession of education; expand the rights and further the interest of educational employees; and advocate human, civil, and economic rights. Its more than 2 million members include elementary and secondary teachers, higher education faculty, educational support personnel, retired educators, and students preparing to become teachers. Contact Allison Kuttner at (202) 822-7440 for more information, or send e-mail to Desperanto@aol.com.

Publications: Offers *Other Ways,* a free resource on violence prevention (available in print or on-line) for everyone working with young people. Includes accepted principles, findings, guidance, and resource information.

National Institute for Dispute Resolution (NIDR)
1726 M Street, NW
Suite 500
Washington, DC 20036-4502
(202) 466-4764
(202) 466-4769 (FAX)
nidr@igc.apc.org

A nonprofit national center of expertise and resources on consensus building and conflict resolution, the NIDR provides technical assistance and coaching, educational programs, consulting, demonstration projects, and evaluations. In 1994, the NIDR initiated an Associates Program that provides dispute resolution practitioners with access to the Institute's collection of resources. Association subscriptions are open to individuals and organizations interested in advancement of the field. In addition, the NIDR partners with a range of organizations that wish to expand the use of consensus-building and conflict resolution tools and techniques in their programs.

Publications: Provides publications such as teaching/training materials and catalogs of conflict resolution books and videos published by the NIDR and others.

National Institute for Violence Prevention (NIVP)
51 Asa Meggs Road
Sandwich, MA 02563
(508) 833-0731

The NIVP is dedicated to the development of expertise and competence in violence prevention strategies among health, education, and human service personnel. It offers professional training programs, workshops, keynote addresses, and technical assistance. Training associates of the NIVP have extensive experience training teachers, youths, public health and medical professionals, criminal justice workers, and social service personnel in the techniques of violence prevention and anger management.

National Rifle Association of America (NRA)
11250 Waples Mill Road
Fairfax, VA 22030
(703) 267-1000

Wayne R. LaPierre, Jr., Executive Director

Formed in 1871, the NRA is the national leader in providing firearms training and gun safety information to the U.S. public. It annually introduces thousands of children from preschool through grade six to the Eddie Eagle Gun Safety Program, which spreads the firearm safety message. Eddie Eagle teaches his young friends to repeat and follow his four-part safety message: *Stop, don't touch, leave the area, tell an adult.* The program was designed in partnership with teachers, school administrators, curriculum and reading specialists, clinical psychologists, law enforcement agents, urban housing safety officials, and NRA firearm safety experts. More than 7 million children since the program's inception in 1988 have had it made available to them.

For more information on the NRA's safety and education programs or publications, contact the Safety and Education Division at (703) 267-1560 or (703) 267-3994 (FAX). For more information on the Eddie Eagle Program, call (800) 231-0752.

Publications: The Eddie Eagle program provides a video, activity books (available in both English and Spanish), and reproducible materials.

National School Boards Association (NSBA)
1680 Duke Street
Alexandria, VA 22314
(703) 838-6722
(703) 838-7590 (FAX)

The NSBA offers information on policies/regulations/laws, gun-related issues, drug-related issues, antiviolence initiatives, school-related initiatives, issues of child victimization, public relations/media strategies, publications, and clearinghouse services/dissemination.

National School Safety Center (NSSC)
Pepperdine University
4165 Thousand Oaks Boulevard
Suite 290
Westlake Village, CA 91362

(805) 373-9977
(805) 373-9277 (FAX)
june@nssc1.org
http://www.nssc1.org
Ronald Stephens, Director

The NSSC is a national clearinghouse for school safety programs and activities related to campus security; school law; community relations; student discipline and attendance; and the prevention of drug abuse, gangs, and bullying. Created in 1984 by presidential mandate through a partnership of the U.S. Department of Justice and the U.S. Department of Education with Pepperdine University, its primary objective is to focus national attention on the importance of providing safe and effective schools.

The NSSC offers print and audiovisual resources, along with on-site training and technical assistance to school districts and law enforcement agencies nationwide. It works with local school districts and communities to develop customized safe school training and planning programs. School districts facing major crises or specific school safety problems may call the center for on-site technical assistance and training.

Publications: The NSSC also serves as a clearinghouse for current information on school safety issues and maintains a resource center with more than 50,000 articles, publications, and films. It publishes numerous publications, including a newsjournal, a newsletter, updates, and special reports, and offers practicums and workshops.

President's Crime Prevention Council
736 Jackson Place, NW
Washington, DC 20503
(202) 395-5555
(202) 395-5567 (FAX)

Also known as the Ounce of Prevention Council, the President's Crime Prevention Council was created by the 1994 Violent Crime Control and Law Enforcement Act. The President's Crime Prevention Council is responsible for developing a catalog of federal prevention programs, coordinating prevention programs and planning across council departments, and assisting communities and community-based organizations in their efforts to prevent crime.

Publications: Among its many projects, the council has developed a catalog entitled *Preventing Crime and Promoting Responsibility: 50 Programs That Help Communities Help Their Youth.* It describes promising youth crime and violence prevention programs sponsored by the federal government, and offers planning information that communities can use to develop a crime prevention effort.

Public Risk Management Association (PRIMA)
1815 Fort Myer Drive
Suite 1020
Arlington, VA 22209
(703) 528-7701
(703) 528-7966 (FAX)
70324.1055@compuserve.com

PRIMA promotes and encourages effective public risk management and risk management professionalism in the public sector and is dedicated to aiding public entities of all types. Through its resources and educational programs, PRIMA helps organizations run their operations more efficiently by applying risk management practices. Membership includes school districts, cities, and counties. Offers publications, annual seminars, an annual conference, information services, state chapter membership, and a network of pools for information exchange. Government, associate, and affiliate memberships are available.

The Center for Public Risk Management, PRIMA's research and data analysis branch, covers the spectrum of risk management issues affecting the public sector. The Speaker's Bureau serves as a referral service for chapters and outside organizations looking for renowned presenters on risk-related topics.

Students against Violence Everywhere (SAVE)
West Charlotte Senior High School
2219 Senior Drive
Charlotte, NC 28216
(714) 343-6060

SAVE is a student-initiated program that teaches elementary and secondary school students gun safety awareness and how to resolve conflict among themselves. It provides education about the effects and consequences of violence, as well as extracurricular activities for students, parents, and the community.

U.S. Department of Education
Office of Special Education and Rehabilitation Services
Office of Special Education Programs
330 C Street, SW
Room 3086, Switzer Building
Washington, DC 20202-2590
(202) 205-5507

The U.S. Department of Education Office of Special Education and Rehabilitation Services provides information about requirements governing disciplining of students covered by the Individuals with Disabilities Education Act (IDEA), and how the requirements of the Gun-Free Schools Act can be applied to students covered by IDEA.

U.S. Department of Education
Safe and Drug-Free Schools Program
600 Independent Avenue, SW
The Portals, Room 604
Washington, DC 20202-6123
(202) 260-3954
(202) 260-7767 (FAX)

The U.S. Department of Education Safe and Drug-Free Schools Program provides information about administration of Safe and Drug-Free Schools Act programs, as well as implementation of the Gun-Free Schools Act. Staff can also help states access PAVNET, an automated clearinghouse that provides information about effective violence prevention programs and strategies.

Regional Centers for Safe and Drug-Free Schools and Communities

Northeast: (516) 589-7022

Serves Connecticut, Delaware, Maine, Maryland, Massachusetts, New Hampshire, New Jersey, New York, Ohio, Pennsylvania, Rhode Island, and Vermont

Southeast: (502) 588-0052

Serves Alabama, District of Columbia, Florida, Georgia, Kentucky, North Carolina, Puerto Rico, South Carolina, Tennessee, the Virgin Islands, Virginia, and West Virginia

Midwest: (708) 571-4710

Serves Illinois, Indiana, Iowa, Michigan, Minnesota, Missouri, Nebraska, North Dakota, South Dakota, and Wisconsin

Southwest: (800) 234-7972

Serves Arizona, Arkansas, Colorado, Kansas, Louisiana, Mississippi, New Mexico, Oklahoma, Texas, and Utah

Western: (503) 275-9480

Serves Alaska, American Samoa, California, Guam, Hawaii, Idaho, Montana, Nevada, the Northern Mariana Islands, Oregon, the Republic of Palau, Washington, and Wyoming

U.S. Department of Health and Human Services
National Clearinghouse on Child Abuse and Neglect
Information
P.O. Box 1182
Washington, DC 20013-1182
(800) 394-3366
(703) 385-3206 (FAX)

The U.S. Department of Health and Human Services National Clearinghouse on Child Abuse and Neglect Information offers information on policies and regulations, drug-related issues, youth-based prevention programs, antiviolence initiatives, school-related initiatives, child victimization issues, community mobilization, statistics and research, public relations/media strategies, training/ technology assistance, publications, program evaluations, and clearinghouse services/dissemination.

U.S. Department of Justice
P.O. Box 6000
Rockville, MD 20849-6000
(800) 638-8736

See Juvenile Justice Clearinghouse (JJC).

WeTip
P.O. Box 1296
Rancho Cucamonga, CA 91729-1296
(909) 987-5005
(909) 987-2475 (FAX)
(800) 782-7463 (Tip Line)

WeTip is a nationwide crime-reporting anonymous tipline that provides 24-hour service, 365 days a year, to take information on all major crimes. Focuses campaigns against youth-related crimes. Holds an annual conference that includes seminars on WeTip and violence-related issues. (For more information on WeTip, see chapter 7.)

Yale School Development Program
Yale University Child Study Center
School Development Program
55 College Street
New Haven, CT 06510
(800) 811-7775
(203) 737-4001 (FAX)

Cynthia Savo, Dissemination and Technology Manager for the School Development Program

See the section entitled "Notable Violence Prevention Curricula and Programs" in chapter 6.

Conferences

National Association for Mediation in Education (NAME) Annual Conference
National Association for Mediation in Education (NAME)
c/o National Institute for Dispute Resolution (NIDR)
1726 M Street, NW
Suite 500
Washington, DC 20036-4502
(202) 466-4764
(202) 466-4769 (FAX)
nidr@igc.apc.org

Annual conference with workshop opportunities for skills development, exploration of emerging issues, and professional development.

National Association of Secondary School Principals (NASSP)
1904 Association Drive
Reston, VA 22091-1537
(703) 860-0200
(703) 476-5432 (FAX)

The NASSP offers an annual convention, along with more than 125 institutes, workshops, and conferences held annually. Provides the opportunity to meet top middle school and high school administrators from across the country to gain new ideas and teaching techniques.

National Crisis Prevention Institute (CPI)
3315-K North 124th Street
Brookfield, WI 53005
(800) 558-8976
(414) 783-5787
(414) 783-5906 (FAX)

The CPI offers an International Instructor's Conference for those certified through the CPI in Nonviolent Crisis Intervention.

Public Risk Management Association (PRIMA) Annual Conference for Public Agencies
1815 Fort Myer Drive
Suite 1020
Arlington, VA 22209
(703) 528-7701
(703) 528-7966 (FAX)

The PRIMA is North America's major annual meeting of government risk managers. Covers current risk-related topics. Each fall, the PRIMA also offers two regional miniconferences that repeat some of the most popular sessions from that year's annual conference. The PRIMA also sponsors an annual Government Risk Management Seminar with intensive workshops and sessions for risk managers of every experience level, covering such topics as safety and loss control, police liability, and general risk management subjects.

Training

The Harvard/EDC Advanced Violence Prevention Training Program for School Professionals
Violence Prevention Programs
Public Health Practice HSPH
718 Huntington Avenue
Boston, MA 02115

(617) 432-2400
jkral@sph.harvard.edu
Jacqueline Kral, Senior Coordinator

The first advanced violence prevention training for school professionals. The program curriculum is based on three graduate-level violence prevention courses at Harvard's School of Public Health and Graduate School of Education and the University of California at Berkeley, which are combined with practitioner-based knowledge. The training addresses critical questions related to the design and implementation of effective programs in schools and communities, and prepares participants to train others. Training topics include multicultural issues, root causes/risk factors, changing school environments, types of violence, and evaluating programs and training. Offered free of charge; a number of limited scholarships may be available.

National Alliance for Safe Schools (NASS)
P.O. Box 1068
College Park, MD 20741
(301) 935-6063
(301) 931-6069 (FAX)

Peter D. Blauvelt, President and CEO

The NASS is a nonprofit corporation founded in 1977 with the purpose of providing technical assistance, training, and research to school districts concerned with increased incidents of serious, disruptive student behavior. It's committed to the beliefs that no child should go to school in fear, and that schools need to take back control and identify the local issues causing fear and anxiety for students and staff.

In addition to a wide range of training, the NASS conducts school security assessments that enable school districts to examine people's perceptions of the seriousness of security incidents in their schools. The assessment also provides the district superintendent with a list of the NASS's findings, as well as recommendations for improvement.

The NASS also assists school districts that want to establish alternative education programs for troubled youth. This ranges from doing preliminary assessments of the community's acceptance of such a program, through selection of site, staff, and students. Extensive training is also available to prepare staff for the unique challenges an alternative program presents.

Violence Prevention Training Institute (VPTI)
School of Professional Psychology
Wright State University
Ellis Human Development Institute
9 North Edwin C. Moses Boulevard
Dayton, OH 45407
(513) 873-4300
(513) 873-4323 (FAX)
W. Rodney Hammond, Ph.D., Project Director

A train-the-trainer institute focusing on violence prevention in the schools. The VPTI will center its continuing education program around the concepts and techniques developed in the Positive Adolescent Choices Training (PACT) program, a school-based violence prevention program model that uses structured pro-social skill development, anger management, and violence risk education to help children and adolescents learn more appropriate and socially effective ways to manage conflict and control strong emotions. The VPTI will prepare 30 child and adolescent service providers to train others in their region to establish and conduct school-based violence prevention programs. Training will take place through the spring of 1997. Selected fellows will travel to Dayton, Ohio, for a week-long residency program of basic training on the PACT model.

Selected Print Resources

Articles

Arbetter, Sandra. **"Violence—A Growing Threat."** *Current Health* 21:6 (February 1995): 6, 7.

A general overview of the probable physiological, sociological, and environmental causes of violence, with emphasis on youth violence.

Coben, Jeffrey H., et al. **"A Primer on School Violence Prevention."** *Journal of School Health* 64:8 (October 1994): 309.

Reviews the problem of violence in public schools and summarizes existing knowledge on school violence prevention, including programs that use educational, regulatory, technological, or combined approaches. Presents recommendations for policy and program needs related to control of school violence.

Dykman, Ann. **"Hardship Duty: A Rising Tide of Youth Violence Has Teachers Worried about the Safety of Their Workplace."** *Techniques* 71:6 (September 1996): 16–23.

Discusses the escalating incidents of violence against teachers, the probable causes of such incidents, and what school systems are doing to prevent them. Includes a survey of vocational educators on school violence.

Elder, R. **"School Environment: Internal and External."** *School Safety* (Fall 1984): 14–16, 23.

Discusses the four elements in the school environment that are necessary for excellence in education: the social, physical, and academic dimensions, and the relationship between law enforcement and the school.

Jackson, Toby. **"The Politics of School Violence."** *Public Interest* 116 (summer 1994): 34–56.

Discusses school violence and how to control it. Argues that teachers maintain order in schools where most students care what teachers think of them. Suggests a "politically incorrect strategy" for controlling school violence: make high school attendance voluntary and require some minimum commitment to educational achievement on the part of all high school students.

Katz, David. **"Training Prevents Violence in Schools, Risk Manager Says."** *National Underwriter* 98:21 (May 23, 1994): 3, 41.

Reports highlights of the annual conference of the Public Risk Management Association, in which risk managers posit that the best way to prevent violence in schools is to train teachers to neutralize student conflicts and show students ways to resolve conflicts peacefully.

Lawton, Millicent. **"Schools Embrace Violence-Prevention Curricula."** *Education Week* 14:10 (November 9, 1994): 1, 10–11.

Gives an overview of the school violence prevention strategies currently in use today, including the most promising interventions.

Posner, Marc. **"Research Raises Troubling Questions about Violence Prevention Programs."** *The Harvard Education Letter* X:3 (May/June 1994): 1–4.

Surfaces issues and questions regarding the efficacy of school violence prevention programs, including whether or not such programs are likely to change complex human behavior. Advises administrators to assess their needs carefully before adopting any program.

————. **"Perception versus Reality: School Uniforms and the 'Halo Effect.'"** *The Harvard Education Letter* XII:3 (May/June 1996): 1–3.

Increasing numbers of U.S. public schools are requiring or promoting the wearing of uniforms. Explores the question of whether uniforms are responsible for the positive effects attributed to them.

Prothrow-Stith, Deborah. **"Building Violence Prevention into the Curriculum."** *The School Administrator* (April 1994): 8–12.

Discusses the need for long-term violence prevention efforts and the components of an ideal school systemwide violence prevention program.

Rosenblatt, Roger. **"Teaching Johnny To Be Good."** The *New York Times* (Magazine) (April 30, 1995): 36–41, 50, 60, 64–65.

Discusses how the character education movement is working to fill what some educators term the "moral vacuum" in which children are now growing up. Gives an overview of the underlying philosophy and history of character education, including the controversy that surrounds it. Discusses instructional strategies used in some character education curriculums, and the problems of deciding which values to teach.

Shanker, Albert. **"Restoring the Connection between Behavior and Consequences."** *Vital Speeches of the Day* 61:15 (May 15, 1995): 463–469.

Discusses the student who is a constant classroom disturbance and thus disrupts the learning environment. Holds that children are deprived of an opportunity to learn if they are not provided with an orderly classroom situation.

Books

Centers for Disease Control and Prevention. **Youth Suicide Prevention Programs: A Resource Guide**. Atlanta: Centers for Disease Control, 1992.

For use by those developing or augmenting suicide prevention programs in their own communities. Details eight suicide prevention strategies: school gatekeeper training, community gatekeeper training, general suicide education, screening programs, peer support programs, crisis centers and hotlines, means restrictions, and intervention after a suicide. Available from the Centers for Disease Control and Prevention, 4770 Buford Highway, NE, Atlanta, GA 30341: (404) 332-4555.

Children's Safety Network. **Taking Action to Prevent Adolescent Violence: Educational Resources for Schools and Community Organizations**. Newton, MA: Children's Safety Network, Adolescent Violence Prevention Resource Center, Education Development Center, June 1995.

Includes summary of promising school-based violence prevention strategies. Also provides an annotated bibliography of more than 80 curricula, a bibliography of more than 150 videos, and other resources. Available from Education Development Center, Inc., 55 Chapel Street, Newton, MA 02158: (800) 225-4276 or (617) 969-7100, ext. 2215.

Comer, James P., et al. **Rallying the Whole Village: The Comer Process for Reforming Education**. New York, NY: Teachers College Press, 1996.

For 25 years, the approach of the Yale School Development Program has been to transform schools into places where students learn, develop, and thrive. This text discusses Comer's holistic model of child development and comprehensive plan for school reform. Topics include children's psychosocial development, group dynamics of effective school communities, teacher preparation and school/university partnerships, appropriate alignment of classroom content to standardized tests, increased student engagement and learning time, research and evaluation, community health, government initiatives, and school/business partnerships.

Greenbaum, Stuart, et al. **Set Straight on Bullies.** Westlake Village, CA: National School Safety Center, 1989.

Examines the bullying problem in the United States and offers strategies for educating the public about bullying and techniques for prevention and intervention to be used by schools. Available from the National School Safety Center, 4165 Thousand Oaks Boulevard, Suite 290, Westlake Village, CA 91362: (805) 373-9977, (805) 373-9277 (FAX).

Lantieri, Linda, and Janet Patti. **Waging Peace in Our Schools**. Boston: Beacon Press, 1996.

Presents information on how the Resolving Conflict Creatively Program (RCCP) has worked and is now serving 325 schools. Describes many examples of how the RCCP has reduced physical violence, fostered appreciation of cultural diversity, enhanced learning, and promoted greater communication between students and teachers, as well as between students both inside and outside school. Includes a history of the RCCP, a working model of the program for professionals who want to adopt it for their schools, and suggestions for parents who want to create "peaceable homes."

National Association of Secondary School Principals. **Safe Schools: A Handbook for Practitioners**. Reston, VA: DynCorp, 1995.

A manual that provides step-by-step instructions on school security and implementing preventive measures. Includes student and staff surveys, policy and program reviews, physical security reviews, school security laws, incident response, techniques for handling the media, and security hardware. Available through the National Association of Secondary School Principals Office of Professional Development: (703) 860-0200 or (800) 253-7746.

National Center for Injury Prevention and Control. **The Prevention of Youth Violence: A Framework for Community Action**. Atlanta, GA: Centers for Disease Control and Prevention, 1993.

A manual for community organizations on organizing activities to prevent youth violence. Includes a menu of specific activities to prevent youth violence, plus a framework for putting those activities in place. Available from the Centers for Disease Control and Prevention, 4770 Buford Highway, NE, Atlanta, GA 30341: (404) 639-3311.

National School Safety Center. **School Safety Check Book**. Westlake Village, CA: National School Safety Center, 1990.

The NSSC's most comprehensive volume on crime and violence prevention in schools. The text is divided into sections on school climate and discipline, school attendance, personal safety, and school security. Geared for the hands-on practitioner, each section includes a review of problems and prevention strategies.

Charts, surveys, and tables, as well as write-ups on a wide variety of model programs, are also included.

Prothrow-Stith, Deborah, with Michael Weissman. **Deadly Consequences: How Violence Is Destroying Our Teenage Population and a Plan to Begin Solving the Problem**. New York: Harper Collins Publishers, 1991.

Looks at various issues of adolescent violence, such as statistical evidence, stages of adolescent development, popular culture, the toll violence takes on male youths of color living in poverty, what children are saying they experience, gangs, drugs, and guns. The authors cite the need for a comprehensive approach to the problem, calling on the public health community, families, schools, and neighborhoods. They discuss the need to mobilize society through its churches, schools, media, government, community organizations, and industry to disseminate the message that anger can be managed and aggressive impulses controlled. Available through the Harvard School of Public Health, 677 Huntington Avenue, Boston, MA 02115 and from HarperCollins, P.O. Box 588, Dunmore, PA 18512: (800) 331-3761.

Rapp, James A., Frank Carrington, and George Nicholson. **School Crime and Violence: Victims' Rights**. Westlake Village, CA: National School Safety Center, 1992.

Comprehensive text on school safety law. Offers a historical overview of victims' rights, describes how they have been dealt with in our laws and courts, and explains their effect on U.S. schools. Authors cite legal case histories and cover current school liability laws. Provides advice to educators and school administrators in risk and liability prevention, and in implementing campus crime prevention programs.

Rosenberg, Mark L., and Mary Ann Fenley, eds. **Violence in America: A Public Health Approach**. Cary, NC: Oxford University Press, 1991.

Updates a series of papers originally prepared for the surgeon general's landmark 1985 Workshop on Violence and Public Health. This comprehensive assessment from a public health perspective describes what is known about different types of violence as well as ways to encourage health professionals' involvement in analysis and action. Chapter topics include child, spouse, and elder abuse; sexual assault and rape; suicide; assaultive violence; and homicide. Each chapter discusses key issues in epidemiology, causes and risk factors, statistical outcomes, and interventions. Available from Oxford University Press, 2001 Evans Road, Cary, NC 27513: (800) 451-7556.

Catalog

President's Crime Prevention Council. **Preventing Crime & Promoting Responsibility: 50 Programs That Help Communities Help Their Youth**. September 1995.

Catalog produced by the President's Crime Prevention Council designed to help communities implement efforts tailored to local resources that prevent youth crime and violence. Includes information on how to develop a comprehensive crime prevention strategy, 50 federal programs that offer financial and technical resources for development and implementation of local solutions, a resource list, selecting reading, and a glossary of federal jargon.

Newsletters

The Fourth R
National Association for Mediation in Education (NAME)
c/o National Institute for Dispute Resolution (NIDR)
1726 M Street, NW
Suite 500
Washington, DC 20036-4502
(202) 466-4764
(202) 466-4769 (FAX)
nidr@igc.apc.org

Keeps members informed about new ideas, programs, events, training, curricula, publications, resources, and teaching methods regarding conflict resolution in education. Published bimonthly. Subscription included with NAME membership: $65 for individuals, $20 for students, $150 for organizations.

NIDR News
National Institute for Dispute Resolution (NIDR)
1726 M Street, NW
Suite 500
Washington, DC 20036-4502
(202) 466-4764
(202) 466-4769 (FAX)
nidr@igc.apc.org

Newsletter for NIDR Associates that reports on the latest developments in the field of dispute resolution, job opportunities, and innovative projects. Published bimonthly. Subscription included with NIDR membership: $75 for individuals, $35 for students, $150 for organizations.

Options
CSN Adolescent Violence Prevention Resource Center
Education Development Center, Inc.
55 Chapel Street
Newton, MA 02158
(617) 969-7100, ext. 2374
(617) 244-3436 (FAX)

For information, contact Ronnie DiComo.

Reports on the science and practice of youth violence prevention. Includes book reviews, resources, news and information, and conferences. Published bimonthly. Call for a free subscription.

Pulse
American School Health Association (ASHA)
7263 State Route 43
P.O. Box 708
Kent, OH 44240
(330) 678-1601
(330) 678-4526 (FAX)

Newsletter for members of the American School Health Association. Published quarterly. Subscription price: included in the ASHA membership of $85.

Riskwatch
Public Risk Management Association (PRIMA)
1815 Fort Myer Drive

Suite 1020
Arlington, VA 22209
(703) 528-7701
(703) 528-7966 (FAX)

PRIMA's newsletter provides a quick review of legislation and current events affecting public agency risk managers. Includes federal and state legislation, insurance issues, court cases, upcoming seminars, meetings, and relevant job openings nationwide. Published monthly. Subscription price: free for members, $125 for nonmembers.

School Safety Update
National School Safety Center (NSSC)
4165 Thousand Oaks Boulevard
Suite 290
Westlake Village, CA 91362
(805) 373-9977
(805) 373-9277 (FAX)

Newsletter of the National School Safety Center. Provides monthly updates from around the country on the most critical issues facing the nation's schools. Also offers insight, strategies, and information on exemplary programs for delinquency prevention and other concerns vital to school safety. Published six times during the school year. A School Safety News Service subscription of $59 includes *School Safety* (NSSC journal) and *School Safety Update*. Current single issues are $6 each; back issues are $9 each.

Urban Educator
Council of the Great City Schools
1301 Pennsylvania Avenue, NW
Suite 702
Washington, DC 20004
(202) 393-2427
(202) 393-2400 (FAX)

Published bimonthly by the Council of the Great City Schools and billed as "the Nation's Voice for Urban Education." Features news and information on legislation, education, and school leadership.

Notable Violence Prevention Curricula and Programs

Aggressors, Victims, and Bystanders
Education Development Center, Inc.
55 Chapel Street
Newton, MA 02158
(617) 969-7101, ext. 2215
(800) 225-4276

For information, contact Millie LeBlanc.

Developed as the result of a three-year research project funded by the Centers for Disease Control and Prevention, this curriculum for students in grades six through nine presents the Think-First Model of conflict resolution. It helps students pause and keep cool, understand the situation before jumping to conclusions, see how bystanders and victims can prevent or escalate a fight, appreciate the perspectives of others, define their problems and goals in ways that will not lead to fights, and generate and act on positive solutions.

The curriculum presents 12 45-minute classroom sessions; provides basic skills training as well as opportunities for youth to develop visions of a nonviolent world; offers teacher background material and student assignments; includes real-life scenarios to use in skill building; and features group discussion, art activities, and role playing.

The curriculum has been extensively field-tested with nearly 700 students in urban, suburban, and small-city school districts.

Developing Personal and Social Responsibility
National School Safety Center (NSSC)
4165 Thousand Oaks Boulevard
Suite 290
Westlake Village, CA 91362
(805) 373-9977
(805) 373-9277 (FAX)

Designed to serve as a framework on which to build successful programs aimed at training young people to be responsible citizens. Based on the premise that schools can play important leadership roles with students, parents, and the community in teaching responsibility skills.

In-Class Curricula for Conflict Resolution
National Association for Mediation in Education (NAME)
c/o National Institute for Dispute Resolution (NIDR)
1726 M Street, NW
Suite 500
Washington, DC 20036-4502
(202) 466-4764
(202) 466-4769 (FAX)
nidr@igc.apc.org

Teaches students the basic concepts of conflict resolution, communication, and problem solving. Teachers are trained to introduce the curriculum to model problem-solving behavior in their classrooms.

Peer Mediation Curricula for Conflict Resolution
National Association for Mediation in Education (NAME)
c/o National Institute for Dispute Resolution (NIDR)
1726 M Street, NW
Suite 500
Washington, DC 20036-4502
(202) 466-4764
(202) 466-4769 (FAX)
nidr@igc.apc.org

Uses trained student mediators to resolve conflicts in a structured, school-based conflict resolution program.

Positive Adolescent Choices Training Program (PACT)
School of Professional Psychology
Wright State University
Ellis Human Development Institute
9 North Edwin C. Moses Boulevard
Dayton, OH 45407
(513) 873-4300
(513) 873-4323 (FAX)

W. Rodney Hammond, Ph.D., Project Director
Trains African-American and other high-risk youth in pro-social and anger management skills. Addresses the problem of expressive violence, which involves loss of control among family, friends, and acquaintances and represents the greatest threat to adolescents. The PACT is one of the few violence prevention programs in the country to have tracked long-term behavioral

outcomes for both its trainees and a comparison group of untrained youth with similar characteristics.

Although developed especially for the needs of African-American youth, the techniques used in the program apply to and are frequently used with multiethnic groups. The program is operated and has been implemented since 1989 in a middle school setting in cooperation with Dayton, Ohio, public schools. The PACT primarily targets high-risk youth between the ages of 12 and 16 who are selected by teachers on the basis of skill deficiencies in relating to peers; behavior problems (particularly aggression); and/or a history of violence, victimization, or exposure.

The Resolving Conflict Creatively Program (RCCP)
National Center
163 Third Avenue, #103
New York, NY 10003
(212) 387-0225
(212) 387-0510 (FAX)
http://www.benjerry.com/esr

For information, contact Linda Lantieri.

Promotes effective instruction in creative conflict resolution and intergroup relations for students in prekindergarten through grade 12. Started in 1985 in New York City, the program is a collaborative effort of the New York City public schools and Educators for Social Responsibility. The objectives of the program include showing young people that they have many choices apart from passivity or aggression for dealing with conflict; giving them the skills to make choices in their own lives; increasing their understanding and appreciation of their own and other cultures; and showing them that they can play a powerful role in creating a more peaceful world.

Core components of the program include a 20-hour training course for teachers, regular classroom instruction in creative conflict resolution and intergroup relations based on a 10-unit curriculum, classroom visits by expert consultants, and monthly two-hour follow-up sessions with teachers in individual schools. Another dimension is peer mediation, in which carefully selected students are trained in mediation skills to serve their schools as playground mediators.

A formal evaluation of the RCCP concluded that teachers who have used this curriculum report fewer fights, less verbal abuse, and more caring behavior on the part of their students. The RCCP is currently the subject of a three-year evaluation funded by the Centers for Disease Control and Prevention.

School-Based Curricula for Conflict Resolution
National Association for Mediation in Education (NAME)
c/o National Institute for Dispute Resolution (NIDR)
1726 M Street, NW
Suite 500
Washington, DC 20036-4502
(202) 466-4764
(202) 466-4769 (FAX)
nidr@igc.apc.org

Responds to conflicts that occur throughout the school. Selected students, teachers, and administrators, trained in conflict resolution and mediation skills, serve as mediators.

Second Step Violence Prevention Curriculum
Committee for Children
2203 Airport Way South
Suite 500
Seattle, WA 98134
(800) 634-4449
(206) 343-1223
(206) 343-1445 (FAX)

For information, contact Client Support Services or Barbara Guzzo.

Addresses the issue of interpersonal violence among children in prekindergarten through eighth grade. It is designed to reduce their impulsive and aggressive behavior and increase their level of social competence through empathy training, interpersonal problem solving, behavior skills training, and anger management. Thus, the curriculum teaches students how to avoid becoming victimizers. Evaluation results of pre- and post-interviews with children who have received the program demonstrate that it had significantly enhanced their empathy, problem-solving, and anger management skills.

Also available is a video-based training program entitled *A Family Guide to Second Step, Parenting Strategies for a Safer Tomorrow*. This component familiarizes parents and caregivers with the Second Step curriculum; helps them reinforce the skills at home; and gives families the skills to communicate feelings, solve problems, control anger, and deal with conflict.

Straight Talk about Risks (STAR)
Center to Prevent Handgun Violence
1225 Eye Street, NW
Suite 1100
Washington, DC 20005
(202) 289-7319

For information, contact Nancy Gannon.

STAR is the nation's first comprehensive, prekindergarten through grade 12 program designed to prevent gunshot injuries and deaths among children and teens by teaching students the protective skills needed to avoid threatening situations with guns. These skills include recognizing danger, critical thinking and decision making, refusal skills to combat negative peer pressure, and conflict resolution skills. The STAR program also seeks to help students develop positive, nonviolent attitudes toward themselves, their peers, and their communities.

The STAR curriculum has evolved from a pilot program implemented in Florida in the Dade County public schools. In the first two years of the Dade County program, there was a 30 percent decrease in gun injuries and deaths among school-aged youth.

The STAR program is available in an integrated bilingual Spanish/English edition.

Violence Prevention Curriculum for Adolescents
Education Development Center, Inc.
55 Chapel Street
Newton, MA 02158
(617) 969-7101, ext. 2215
(800) 225-4276

For information, contact Millie LeBlanc.

A ten-session course for students in grades 9–12 that addresses violence and homicide among young people. It is part of the Teenage Health Teaching Modules program, the only nationally evaluated comprehensive school health education curriculum for adolescents. The violence prevention curriculum acknowledges anger as a normal and natural emotion and provides facts that alert students to their high risk of being either the victim or the perpetrator of an act of violence. It creates a need in students to find alternatives to fighting by discussing the potential gains and losses, offers positive ways to deal with anger and arguments, and allows students to analyze the precursors of a fight and to practice conflict resolution through role-playing and videotaping.

An evaluation funded by the National Institute of Justice demonstrated that the curriculum had positive impacts on students in four urban high schools across the country. Students who received the curriculum reported having fewer fights and arrests, and had higher scores of a measure of self-esteem.

The curriculum was developed by Deborah Prothrow-Stith, M.D., assistant dean for Government and Community Programs at the Harvard School of Public Health, and the Education Development Center in Newton, Massachusetts. It can be incorporated into high school health, sociology, psychology, and other classes. It is also suitable for use outside the classroom (for example, in alternative schools, recreational programs, public housing developments, Sunday schools, and neighborhood health centers of YMCAs).

Yale School Development Program
Yale University Child Study Center
School Development Program
55 College Street
New Haven, CT 06510
(800) 811-7775
(203) 737-4001 (FAX)

For information, contact Cynthia Savo, Dissemination and Technology Manager.

The mission of the School Development Program is to bring together teachers, administrators, students, and parents to develop a comprehensive plan of social and academic goals to help change the culture of a school. The program now operates in more than 600 schools. Although it originally addressed the needs of urban students and schools, it is now being implemented in a broad array of diverse communities.

Studies conducted to assess the effects of the program on student and teacher outcomes and general school climate changes indicate that the program has a significant positive effect on student achievement, self-esteem, and overall adjustment. The data also show that parents feel more connected to their children's schools and that teachers have increased feelings of satisfaction with their work.

The program also provides information and assistance to help schools of education, state education departments, and other agencies make their policies and practices more child centered.

Papers

Elliott, Delbert. **"Youth Violence: An Overview."** In Clark, Dick, ed. **Children and Violence**. Queenstown, MD: The Aspen Institute, February 18–21, 1994.

Considers current patterns and trends of youth violence, causes of youth violence, and what is known about the prevention of youth violence. Available from the Center for the Study and Prevention of Violence (CSPV), University of Colorado at Boulder, Campus Box 442, Boulder, CO 80309-0442, (303) 492-8465, (303) 443-3297 (FAX).

Maxwell, Christopher, and Sheila Royo Maxwell. **"Adolescent Involvement in Violent Hate Crimes."**

Includes a review of what is known about adolescent involvement in violent hate crimes, what appears to be known yet has limitations, and gaps in research and knowledge. Hate crimes with regard to race, ethnicity, sexual orientation, religion, and the disabled and disfigured population are examined on a national and local level. Available from the Center for the Study and Prevention of Violence (CSPV), University of Colorado at Boulder, Campus Box 442, Boulder, CO 80309-0442, (303) 492-8465, (303) 443-3297 (FAX).

Osgood, D. Wayne. **"Drugs, Alcohol, and Adolescent Violence."**

Critical review of the literature that includes a review of what is known about drugs, alcohol, and adolescent violence; what appears to be known yet has limitations; and gaps in research and knowledge. Available from the Center for the Study and Prevention of Violence (CSPV), University of Colorado at Boulder, Campus Box 442, Boulder, CO 80309-0442, (303) 492-8465, (303) 443-3297 (FAX).

Tolan, Patrick, and Nancy Guerra. **"What Works in Reducing Adolescent Violence: An Empirical Review of the Field."**

Examines the effectiveness of juvenile violence prevention and treatment programs. Reviews program evaluations and other research literature focusing on program effectiveness as it relates to adolescent violence prevention and treatment. Available from the Center for the Study and Prevention of Violence (CSPV),

University of Colorado at Boulder, Campus Box 442, Boulder, CO 80309-0442, (303) 492-8465, (303) 443-3297 (FAX).

Wilson-Brewer, Renee, Stu Cohen, Lydia O'Donnell, and Irene F. Goodman. **"Violence Prevention for Young Adolescents: A Survey of the State of the Art."** September 1991.

Revised version of the working paper prepared by the Education Development Center for the conference "Violence Prevention for Young Adolescents," which was held in Washington, D.C., on 12–13 July 1980, supported by the Carnegie Corporation of New York.

Available from the ERIC Clearinghouse, ERIC Customer Service, (800) 443-3742.

Periodicals

Below are some of the leading publications in health, education, and conflict resolution that frequently carry articles related to youth violence, school violence, and school safety.

Education Week
Editorial Projects in Education Inc.
4301 Connecticut Avenue, NW
Suite 250
Washington, DC 20008
(202) 364-4114
(202) 364-1039 (FAX)
ew@epe.org

Reports on education-related issues and resources. An excellent resource for user-friendly information on school violence issues, including prevention programs, updates on statistics, and public policy. Published weekly (41 issues). Subscription price: $69.94 for one year, $115 for two years, $159 for three years.

Forum
National Institute for Dispute Resolution (NIDR)
1726 M Street, NW
Suite 500
Washington, DC 20036-4502
(202) 466-4764
(202) 466-4769 (FAX)
nidr@igc.apc.org

Informs and stimulates debate about the use of conflict resolution procedures. Published three times a year. Subscription included in NIDR membership: $75 for individuals, $35 for students, $150 for organizations.

The Harvard Education Letter
Gutman Library
6 Appian Way
Cambridge, MA 02138-3752
(617) 495-3432
(617) 496-3584 (FAX)

Frequently runs thought-provoking articles about school-related issues such as school uniforms and the efficacy of school violence prevention programs. Published bi-monthly. Subscription price: $26 per year.

Health Affairs
Project HOPE
7500 Old Georgetown Road
Suite 600
Bethesda, MD 20814
(301) 656-7401
(301) 654-2845 (FAX)

Reports on issues related to public health policy. The winter 1993 issue (12:4) is dedicated to violence prevention and is available for $25. Published six times each year. Subscription price: $79 for individuals, $129 for institutions.

Journal of Safe Management and Disruptive and Assaultive Behavior (JSM)
National Crisis Prevention Institute (CPI)
3315-K North 124th Street
Brookfield, WI 53005
(800) 558-8976
(414) 783-5787
(414) 783-5906 (FAX)

The CPI's journal, which offers a collection of articles on violence prevention strategies. Also offers an additional publication entitled the *Instructor Forum*. Both are available free with CPI training certification. Published quarterly. Subscription price: $45 for one year, $70 for two years, $90 for three years.

Journal of School Health
American School Health Association (ASHA)
7263 State Route 43
P.O. Box 708
Kent, OH 44240
(330) 678-1601
(330) 678-4526 (FAX)

Professional journal published by the ASHA on topical issues related to the health of school children. Published monthly during the school year. Subscription price: $120 a year.

Morbidity and Mortality Weekly Report
Centers for Disease Control and Prevention
4770 Buford Highway, NE
Atlanta, GA 30341
(404) 639-3311

Publishes violence statistics on both youth and adults. Published weekly. Subscription price: $89 a year. Contact the Massachusetts Medical Society at 1-800-843-6356 for more information on this publication.

Public Risk
Public Risk Management Association (PRIMA)
1815 Fort Myer Drive
Suite 1020
Arlington, VA 22209
(703) 528-7701
(703) 528-7966 (FAX)

The PRIMA magazine, which provides news and features on risk management. Each issue contains technical and how-to articles on risk management subjects. Regular departments cover pooling issues, legislative news, chapter affairs, and Association news. Published monthly. Subscription price: free for members, $125 for nonmembers.

School Safety
National School Safety Center (NSSC)
4165 Thousand Oaks Boulevard
Suite 290
Westlake Village, CA 91362
(805) 373-9977
(805) 373-9277 (FAX)

Newsjournal of the National School Safety Center. Published quarterly. A School Safety News Service subscription of $59 includes *School Safety* and *School Safety Update* (NSSC newsletter). Current single issues are $9 each; back issues are $12 each.

Reports

Council of the Great City Schools. **"Caring Schools, Caring Communities: An Urban Blueprint for Comprehensive School Health and Safety."** January 1994.

Describes proceedings from a December 1993 symposium on urban school reform, health, and safety that define the magnitude of unsafe conditions in urban schools and presents successful school health and violence prevention programs. Fifty-four educators, health professionals, and leaders from community programs and national coalitions offer views on the causes of school violence and how communities can help to remedy growing threats to student well-being. Available from Council of the Great City Schools, 1301 Pennsylvania Avenue, NW, Suite 702, Washington, DC 20004: (202) 393-2427, (202) 393-2400 (FAX).

Mendel, Richard A. **"Prevention or Pork? A Hard-Headed Look at Youth-Oriented Anti-Crime Programs."** Washington, DC: American Youth Policy Forum, 1995.

Summarizes what is known from research and evaluation about the effectiveness of the types of youth-oriented crime prevention strategies that might be supported under the Violent Crime Control and Law Enforcement Act of 1994. Available from American Youth Policy Forum, 1001 Connecticut Avenue, NW, Suite 719, Washington, DC 20036-5541.

National Education Goals Panel. **"National Education Goals Report, Executive Summary: Improving Education through Family-School-Community Partnerships."** Washington, DC, 1995.

A condensation of the information contained in the 1995 National Education Goals Report, which is fifth in a series of annual reports that discusses the progress made toward the National Education Goals through 2000. Available from the National Education Goals Panel, 1255 22nd Street, NW, Suite 502, Washington, DC 20037: (202) 632-0952, (202) 632-0957 (FAX).

National School Safety Center. **"School Safety, Alternative Education: A Road toward Success for Troubled Youth."** Winter 1995.

Discusses alternative opportunities for youth who do not perform well in traditional school settings, especially disruptive youth. Available from the National School Safety Center, 4165 Thousand Oaks Boulevard, Suite 290, Westlake Village, CA 91362, (805) 373-9977, (805) 373-9277 (FAX).

Office of Drug-Free Schools. **"Success Stories '94: A Guide to Safe, Disciplined, and Drug-Free Schools."** 1994.

Offers practical advice from educators, parents, and community leaders on building the six key components of a sound, comprehensive prevention program. Available from the U.S. Department of Education, 330 C Street, SW, Room 3086, Switzer Building, Washington, DC 20202-2590: (202) 205-5507.

Snyder, Howard N., and Melissa Sickmund. **"Juvenile Offenders and Victims: A National Report."** Washington, DC: Office of Juvenile Justice and Delinquency Prevention, 1995.

An excellent reference document that consolidates the most requested information on juvenile offenders and victims in a user-friendly format. Available from Juvenile Justice Clearinghouse, P.O. Box 6000, Rockville, MD 20849-6000: (800) 638-8736 or look@ncjrs.aspensys.com.

U.S. General Accounting Office. **"School Safety: Promising Initiatives for Addressing School Violence."** Washington, DC: U.S. General Accounting Office (Health, Education, and Human Services Division), April 1995.

Gives information about some of the programs used by schools to curb violence. Examines four promising prevention programs, includes teacher and student views on these efforts, and reviews evaluation data on these programs. Identifies key characteristics typically associated with promising school-based violence prevention programs. Also identifies federally sponsored evaluations of school violence prevention programs. Available from U.S. General Accounting Office, P.O. Box 6015, Gaithersburg, MD 20884-6015: (202) 512-6000, (301) 258-4066 (FAX), or (301) 413-0006 (TDD).

Surveys

American School Health Association. **"The National Adolescent Student Health Survey: A Report on the Health of America's Youth."** Oakland, CA: Third Party Publishing, 1989.

Available from the American School Health Association, 7263 State Route 43, P.O. Box 708, Kent, OH 44240: (330) 678-1601, (330) 678-5626 (FAX).

Carnegie Corporation. **"Saving Youth from Violence."**

Available from Carnegie Corporation of New York, 437 Madison Avenue, New York, NY 10022.

Children's Defense Fund. **"Annual Report: State of America's Children."**

Available from the Children's Defense Fund Publications Department, 25 E Street, NW, Washington, DC 20001: (202) 628-8787.

Council of the Great City Schools. **"Urban School Safety: Strategies of the Great City Schools."** March 1994.

Efforts of 38 large urban school districts to provide safe conditions for their students are compiled in this district-by-district narrative of preventive and intervention programs. Conflict resolution curricula, metal detectors, police patrols, and programs aimed at educating students about drug abuse, resisting peer pressure, and legal penalties for unlawful behavior are among the strategies prescribed to respond to violent environments in and around school campuses. Available from Council of the Great City Schools, 1301 Pennsylvania Avenue, NW, Suite 702, Washington, DC 20004: (202) 393-2427, (202) 393-2400 (FAX).

Harris, L. and Associates, Inc. **"The Metropolitan Life Survey of the American Teacher."**

An annual survey sponsored by MetLife that explores teacher's opinions and brings them to the attention of the U.S. public and policymakers. The 1994 *Survey*, for example, explored "Violence in America's Public Schools: The Family Perspective." The survey is based on 15-minute telephone interviews with a nationally representative sample of public school teachers. Available from

MetLife, The American Teacher Survey, P.O. Box 807, Madison Square Station, New York, NY 10159-0807.

"Keeping Our Schools Safe: A Survey of Teachers and Students about Violence in U.S. Schools."

Available from Lynne Warne, marketing communications manager, Honeywell Inc., Honeywell Plaza, P.O. Box 524, Minneapolis, MN 55408: (612) 951-2296.

U.S. Department of Justice. **"School Crime."**

Available from U.S. Department of Justice, Office for Victims of Crime Resource Center, P.O. Box 6000, Rockville, MD 20850: (800) 627-8787.

Selected Nonprint Resources

Databases/Online Services/ World Wide Web Sites

Databases

CDC Wonder
Centers for Disease Control and Prevention (CDC)
4770 Buford Highway, NE
Atlanta, GA 30341
(404) 332-4555
http://wonder.cdc.gov

Provides query access to some 40 text-based numeric databases that contain information such as CDC reports and guidelines, as well as numeric public health data. (For example, users can request data for any disease and demographic group.) Also provides search and retrieval for important texts such as the *Morbidity and Mortality Weekly Report*. (For more information on the Centers for Disease Control and Prevention, see chapter 5 and the CDC Web site below.)

Speakers Bureau Database
Public Risk Management Association (PRIMA)
1815 Fort Myer Drive

Suite 1020
Arlington, VA 22209
(703) 528-7701
(703) 528-7966 (FAX)

PRIMA's Speakers Bureau Database contains information about well-known presenters on risk-related topics, their areas of expertise, and evaluations from previous speaking engagements. (For more information on PRIMA, see chapter 5.)

VioLit/VioPro/VioSource/VioEval/VioClip Databases
Center for the Study and Prevention of Violence (CSPV)
Institute of Behavioral Science
University of Colorado at Boulder
Campus Box 442
Boulder, CO 80309-0442
(303) 492-8465
(303) 443-3297 (FAX)
cspv@colorado.edu
http://www.colorado.edu/cspv

Through the CSPV's Information House, violence-related research information is collected, summarized, evaluated, and stored in the VioLit database. The research abstracts are important because the quality of studies varies widely; not all findings are of equal importance for designing programs, establishing policy, or stimulating research. Information House offers free topical database searches and provides bibliographic information, abstracts, and references to literature.

Information House also maintains four other databases:

VioPro, the program database, provides information on violence prevention, intervention, and treatment programs. Topical searches generate listings of program names, addresses, phone numbers, and brief program descriptions.

VioSource, the resource database, maintains reference information regarding resource materials on violence and violence prevention. Information regarding resource location is included with each reference. Brief descriptions of VioSource material are also included when available.

VioEval, the survey and evaluation instrument database, stores information about survey instruments designed to measure violence-related behaviors and attitudes. When available from the author, instruments are kept on file at the CSPV and provided to Information House customers upon request. Specific questions about particular instruments are addressed directly to the authors.

VioClip, the newspaper/magazine database, is a compilation of newspaper and magazine articles on subjects in the area of violence and prevention. This database contains articles that reference the CSPV or CSPV staff members and articles that have been brought to the attention of the Information House staff.

Free customized topical searches from all CSPV databases are available to the public. (For more information on CSPV, see chapter 5 and the section on Web sites below.)

Online Services

Adolescence Directory Online (ADOL)
The Center for Adolescent Studies—Indiana University
http://education.indiana.edu/cas/adol/adol.html

A service of the Center for Adolescent Studies at Indiana University, the ADOL is an electronic guide to information on adolescent issues for educators, counselors, parents, researchers, health practitioners, and teens. The ADOL includes resources about violence prevention and peer mediation, information on mental health issues related to the psychological well-being of teens, information on health risks, and counselor resources. (See Teacher Talk Forum under Web sites below.)

PAVNET (Partnerships against Violence Network) Federal Online Service
National Institute of Justice
Washington, DC 20531
For more information, contact:
National Criminal Justice Reference Service (NCJRS)
P.O. Box 6000
Rockville, MD 20849-6000
(800) 851-3420
(301) 251-5212 (FAX)
http:www.askncjrs@ncjrs.aspensys.com

The PAVNET online service contains more than 600 descriptions of promising violence prevention programs. It also provides information on technical assistance to organizations regarding violence-related problems and on planning and implementing programs to prevent or reduce violence. It includes descriptions of curricula and teaching materials, and contact information for ordering the texts, manuals, videotapes, or other materials. It provides information on funding for violence prevention and violence reduction programs available from federal agencies and private foundations. The PAVNET is also available in a two-volume resource guide and on diskette. (For more information on the NCJRS, see chapter 5 and the Web site for the NCJRS below.)

World Wide Web Sites

The Center for the Study and Prevention of Violence (CSPV)
Institute for Behavioral Science
University of Colorado at Boulder
Campus Box 442
Boulder, CO 80309-0442
(303) 492-8465
(303) 443-3297 (FAX)
cspv@colorado.edu
http://www.colorado.edu/cspv

Provides access to information on and resources available through the CSPV (for example, databases, publications, and speakers), current research projects conducted by the Center, and other violence prevention resources available on the Internet. (For more information on the CSPV, see chapter 5. Also see the listing for the VioLit/VioPro/VioSource/VioEval/VioClip databases above.)

Centers for Disease Control and Prevention (CDC)
4770 Buford Highway, NE
Atlanta, GA 30341
(404) 639-3311
http://www.cdc.gov

Provides access to overview information on the CDC as well as access to health information, publications and products, data and statistics, training and employment, and funding. (For more information on the Centers for Disease Control and Prevention, see chapter 5 and the listing for CDC Wonder under databases above.)

Character Education Partnership (CEP)
809 Franklin Street
Alexandria, VA 22314-4105
(800) 988-8081
(703) 739-9515
(703) 739-4967 (FAX)
geninfo@character.org
http://web2010.com/cepweb

Provides access to information on character education, such as articles, resources, and organizations that provide character education materials; on what concerned citizens can do; on the CEP Annual Forum; and on the 11 principles of effective character education. (For more information on the CEP, see chapter 5.)

Education Development Center (EDC)
55 Chapel Street
Newton, MA 02160
(617) 969-7100
(617) 244-3436 (FAX)
http://www.edc.org/home.html

Provides access to information on the EDC's products, history, and current work in injury and violence prevention and control, as well as updates on progress in its quest to help reduce violence across the life cycle. (For more information on the EDC, see chapter 5. Also see the Web site for the National Network of Violence Prevention Practitioners below.)

National Clearinghouse for Alcohol and Drug Information
webmaster@health.org
http://www.health.org

Provides access to resources and referrals, research and statistics, information about online forums, a conference calendar, and related Internet links. The National Clearinghouse for Alcohol and Drug Information PREVLINE offers access to databases and substance abuse prevention materials that pertain to alcohol, tobacco, and drugs.

National Criminal Justice Reference Service (NCJRS)
P.O. Box 6000
Rockville, MD 20849-6000
(800) 851-3420
(301) 251-5500
http:www.look@ncjrs.aspensys.com

Provides access to information from the NCJRS, one of the most extensive sources of information on criminal and juvenile justice in the world. The NCJRS is a collection of clearinghouses supporting all bureaus of the U.S. Department of Justice, Office of Justice Programs (OJP): the National Institute of Justice, the Office of Juvenile Justice and Delinquency Prevention, the Bureau of Justice Statistics, the Bureau of Justice Assistance, the Office for Victims of Crime, the OJP Program Offices, and the Office of National Drug Control Policy. The NCJRS Web site provides access to such information as criminal justice statistics, juvenile justice, research and evaluation, conferences, grants, and factoids on criminal justice. (For more information on the NCJRS, see the Juvenile Justice Clearinghouse in chapter 5.)

National Education Association of the United States (NEA)
1201 16th Street, NW
Washington, DC 20036-3290
(202) 833-4000
http://www.nea.org

Provides access to information on the NEA and public education in the United States, as well as information that "can help public education work for every child and every family," such as technology in the classroom and tips and ideas for helping students learn. (For more information on the NEA, see chapter 5.)

National Network of Violence Prevention Practitioners (NNVPP)
55 Chapel Street
Newton, MA 02160
(617) 969-7100
(617) 244-3436 (FAX)
http://www.edc.org/HHD/NNVPP

The NNVPP is composed of members dedicated to violence prevention among our nation's youth. The Web site provides access to information about the network, upcoming conferences, member information, sample materials, the Educational Development Center violence prevention products, a membership application, and hotlinks to other organizations. (For more information on the NNVPP, see the Education Development Center in chapter 5 and the Web site for the EDC above.)

Teacher Talk Forum Lesson Plans
Center for Adolescent Studies—Indiana University
http://education.indiana.edu/cas/ttforum/lesson.html

A service of the Center for Adolescent Studies at Indiana University, this Web site offers interdisciplinary lesson plans on violence prevention for art, health education, language arts, mathematics, and social studies classes. (See Adolescence Directory Online [ADOL] under Online Services above.)

U.S. Department of Education
Washington, DC 20202
http://www.ed.gov

Provides access to updates on such key educational initiatives as Goals 2000 and the Department of Education budget; resources the Department makes available to teachers, researchers, and students; press releases; transcripts of speeches and testimony made by the secretary of education; information on grant applications; new funding opportunities; programs available in each state; publications and products; and links to other public sites of interest. (For more information on the Department of Education, see chapter 5.)

Films and Videotapes

Alternatives to Violence: Conflict Resolution, Negotiation, and Mediation

Type:	videocassette
Length:	30 min. each (two)
Date:	1994
Cost:	$150
Source:	Chariot Productions
	2819 Third Street
	Boulder, CO 80304
	(800) 477-5128
	(303) 786-9799 (FAX)

Developed to help educators teach students in grades 6–12 the concepts and skills they need for productive conflict resolution. Part 1 shows students the value of conflict resolution as an alternative to fighting. Part 2 covers the value of teaching students conflict resolution skills and discusses how to implement and run a school-based conflict resolution and mediation program.

Anger: You Can Handle It

Type:	videocassette
Length:	25 min.
Date:	1995
Cost:	$169.95

Source: Sunburst Communications
39 Washington Avenue
P.O. Box 40
Pleasantville, NY 10570
(800) 431-1934
(914) 769-2109 (FAX)

An anger management video for students in grades 7–12. A teacher's guide is included.

Beginning with the Children: A National Teleconference on Violence Prevention
Type: videocassette
Length: 50 min.
Date: 1993
Cost: $25
Source: Resolving Conflict Creatively Program
163 Third Avenue, #239
New York, NY 10003
(212) 387-0225
(212) 387-0510 (FAX)
http://www.benjerry.com/esr

Shows adults and youth exchanging ideas about conflict resolution programs in New York City, Philadelphia, Washington, D.C., and Dallas schools.

Conflict Resolution Curriculum Module: Grades 2–5
Type: videocassettes ($649 for all seven)

All about Anger
Length: 15 min.
Date: 1991
Cost: $99.95

Getting Better at Getting Along
Length: 16 min.
Date: 1996
Cost: $114.95

It's Not Fair
Length: 14 min.
Date: 1993
Cost: $99.95

Respect Yourself and Others Too
Length: 17 min.
Date: 1996
Cost: $114.95

Students Workshop: Solving Conflicts
Length: 26 min.
Date: 1994
Cost: $129.95

Staff Development on Self-Esteem
Length: 29 min.
Date: 1995
Cost: $149.95

Conflict Resolution for Elementary Grades
Length: 29 min.
Date: 1995
Cost: $149.95
Source: Sunburst Communications
39 Washington Avenue
P.O. Box 40
Pleasantville, NY 10570-0040
(800) 431-1934
(914) 769-2109 (FAX)

Includes five student videos, two staff development videos, a 175-page teacher's guide, 30 activity sheets, 20 activity cards, 20 "What If?" cards, four information sheets, six family activity sheets, four posters, and a storage box.

Conflict Resolution Curriculum Module: Grades 5–9
Type: videocassettes ($749 for all six)

Working It Out
Length: 28 min.
Date: 1992
Cost: $189.95

Between You and Me
Length: 20 min.
Date: 1991
Cost: $149.95

Me and My Parents
Length: 23 min.
Date: 1991
Cost: $169.95

When You're Mad! Mad! Mad!
Length: 27 min.
Date: 1993
Cost: $169.95

Student Workshop: Conflict Resolution
Length: 35 min.
Date: 1993
Cost: $199.95

Staff Development: Conflict Resolution for Grades 5–12
Length: 24 min.
Date: 1992
Cost: $149.95
Source: Sunburst Communications
39 Washington Avenue
P.O. Box 40
Pleasantville, NY 10570-0040
(800) 431-1934
(914) 769-2109 (FAX)

Includes five student videos, one staff development video, a 125-page teacher's guide, ten information sheets, 24 activity sheets, 20 activity cards, 24 role-play cards, four posters, and a storage box.

Conflict Resolution Curriculum Module: Grades 9–12
Type: videocassettes ($749 for all five)

Student Workshop: Mediation
Length: 24 min.
Date: 1995
Cost: $149.95

Conflict Resolution
Length: 26 min.
Date: 1992
Cost: $169.95

Student Workshop: Resolving Conflicts
Length: 24 min.
Date: 1994
Cost: $199.95

Anger: You Can Handle It
Length: 24 min.
Date: 1995
Cost: $169.95

Teen–Parent Conflict
Length: 29 min.
Date: 1995
Cost: $149.95

Source: Sunburst Communications
39 Washington Avenue
P.O. Box 40
Pleasantville, NY 10570-0040
(800) 431-1934
(914) 769-2109 (FAX)

Includes four student videos, one staff development video, a 130-page teacher's guide, 24 activity sheets, 16 activity cards, 24 role-play cards, 45 image cards, 11 information sheets, four posters, and a storage box.

Coping with Fighters, Bullies, and Troublemakers
Type: videocassette
Length: 22 min.
Date: 1992
Cost: $89
Source: Bureau of Violence Prevention
NIMCO, Inc.
117 Highway
P.O. Box 9
Calhoun, KY 42327-0009
(800) 962-6662
(502) 273-5844 (FAX)

Offers students specific techniques for coping with disruptive classmates.

Dealing with Anger: A Violence Prevention Program for African-American Youth
Type: videocassettes ($740 for all six)

Videos for Males (three videos)
Length: 52 min. (total running time for 3 videos)
Date: 1991
Cost: $495

Videos for Females (three videos)
Length: 68 min. (total running time for 3 videos)
Date: 1994
Cost: $495
Source: Research Press
P.O. Box 9177
Champaign, IL 61826
(217) 352-3273
(217) 352-1221 (FAX)

A video-based training program developed in response to the need for culturally relevant materials to train African-American youth in skills that will reduce their disproportionate risk of becoming victims or perpetrators of violence. The program is built around three instructional videotapes; the on-screen narrator prepares viewers for each scene and follows up with comments on what went right or wrong. Videos include footage of group training sessions in which adolescents discuss conflict situations, learn skills for resolving these conflicts, role-play some of the situations, and give/receive feedback on their role-play performances. Training package also includes a Leader's Guide and Skill Cards (student handouts that list the steps for each skill and serve as prompts for quick reference during training).

Learning To Manage Anger: The RETHINK Workout for Teens
Type: videocassette
Length: 33 min.
Date: 1988
Cost: $200
Source: Research Press
P.O. Box 9177
Champaign, IL 61826
(217) 352-3273
(217) 352-1221 (FAX)

Teaches junior high and high school students to control anger and resolve conflict through the seven-step RETHINK method.

Listening to Children: A Moral Journey with Robert Coles
Type: videocassette
Length: 90 min.
Date: 1995
Cost: $69.95
Source: PBS Video
Public Broadcasting Service
1320 Braddock Place
Alexandria, VA 22314-1698
(800) 344-3337

How does a child grow up to become a moral adult? Pulitzer Prize-winning author and child psychiatrist Robert Coles explores why some children lead lives guided by a strong conscience while others do not. The program looks at how parents, teachers, and caring adults pass on a moral inheritance to children and give them the psychological foundation they need to grow into responsible, compassionate people. Includes a 24-page discussion guide for parents, caregivers, and teachers.

Making a Difference

Type: videocassette
Length: 26 min.
Date: 1993
Cost: $25
Source: Educators for Social Responsibility (ESR)
            23 Garden Street
            Cambridge, MA 02138
            (800) 370-2515
            (617) 492-1764
            (617) 864-5164 (FAX)
            http://www.benjerry.com/esr

The Resolving Conflict Creatively Program is the basis of this video, which looks at the changes that occur in students and teachers when peer mediation and conflict resolution programs are implemented.

Peacemakers of the Future

Type: videocassette
Length: 23 min.
Date: NA
Cost: NA
Source: National Association for Mediation in Education
            (NAME)
            c/o National Institute for Dispute Resolution (NIDR)
            1726 M Street, NW
            Suite 500
            Washington, DC 20036-4502
            (202) 466-4764
            (202) 466-4769 (FAX)
            nidr@igc.apc.org

Documents the changes that occur as the result of a mediation program for elementary school students and follows the students as they move into middle school and high school. Shows ways a mediation program can be integrated into an elementary school curriculum and how students can apply its principles.

Resolving Conflicts through Mediation

Type: videocassette
Length: 8 min.

Date: NA
Cost: NA
Source: National Association for Mediation in Education
(NAME)
c/o National Institute for Dispute Resolution (NIDR)
1726 M Street, NW
Suite 500
Washington, DC 20036-4502
(202) 466-4764
(202) 466-4769 (FAX)
nidr@igc.apc.org

For kindergarten through grade 6. Contains dramatized situations of student conflicts. Shows how other students in peer mediator roles help resolve disputes on the playground, at lunch, and on the school bus.

School Crisis: Under Control
Type: videocassette
Length: 25 min.
Date: 1991
Cost: $75
Source: National School Safety Center (NSSC)
4165 Thousand Oaks Boulevard
Suite 290
Westlake Village, CA 91362
(805) 373-9977
(805) 373-9277 (FAX)

Actor Edward James Olmos hosts this documentary. It combines actual news footage of school crisis events and features participants at the National School Safety Center's "School Crisis Prevention Practicum" offering educators advice about school crisis prevention, preparation, management, and resolution. Covers topics such as outlining staff roles and responsibilities, dealing with the media, providing adequate communication systems and signals, arranging transportation, and offering grief counseling.

School Violence: Answers from the Inside
Type: videocassette
Length: 30 min.
Date: 1995
Cost: $59.95

Source: PBS Video
            Public Broadcasting Service
            1320 Braddock Place
            Alexandria, VA 22314-1698
            (800) 344-3337

Profiles teens and schools that have discovered some answers to school violence. Closed-captioned for the hearing impaired. Includes teacher resource material.

Set Straight on Bullies
Type: 16mm color film or videocassette
Length: 18 min.
Date: 1988
Cost: $75
Source: National School Safety Center (NSSC)
           4165 Thousand Oaks Boulevard
           Suite 290
           Westlake Village, CA 91362
           (805) 373-9977
           (805) 373-9277 (FAX)

Produced to help school administrators educate faculty, parents, and students about the severity of the schoolyard bullying problem. Tells the dramatic story of a bullying victim and how the problems adversely affect his life, as well as the lives of the bully, other students, parents, and educators.

Teen Violence
Type: videocassette
Length: 30 min.
Date: 1993
Cost: $69.95
Source: PBS Video
           Public Broadcasting Service
           1320 Braddock Place
           Alexandria, VA 22314-1698
           (800) 344-3337

Explores how teens deal with violence and potentially explosive situations, and the role adults can play in helping young people deal with violence as an everyday fact of life. Includes an in-depth discussion with high school students.

Understanding and Resolving Conflicts
Type: videocassette
Length: 20 min.
Date: 1994
Cost: $95
Source: United Learning
6633 West Howard Street
P.O. Box 48718
Niles, IL 60714-0718
(800) 424-0362
(708) 647-0918 (FAX)

For middle school and high school students. Explains how and why conflict occurs and gives a problem-solving approach to resolving it. Role-playing illustrates the characteristics of conflict and demonstrates resolution techniques.

Violence Prevention
Type: videocassette
Length: 30 min.
Date: 1994
Cost: $59.95
Source: PBS Video
Public Broadcasting Service
1320 Braddock Place
Alexandria, VA 22314-1698
(800) 344-3337

Teens discuss friends they have lost to street violence. A teen shooting victim talks about surviving gun-related violence. Teens at one urban high school combat the violence in their community by teaching antiviolence counseling. The program includes an appearance by rap artist D. J. Jazzy Jeff and the Fresh Prince. Closed-captioned for the hearing impaired.

What's Wrong with This Picture?
Type: 16mm color film or videocassette
Length: 18 min.
Date: 1986
Cost: $50
Source: National School Safety Center (NSSC)
4165 Thousand Oaks Boulevard
Suite 290
Westlake Village, CA 91362

(805) 373-9977
(805) 373-9277 (FAX)

A docudrama showing five scenarios that address the school safety issues of drug trafficking and abuse, intimidation and violence, teacher burnout, and theft. Narrated by people who actually experienced the incidents portrayed, this film is intended to generate emotional responses, discussions, and action from its viewers.

Who Cares about Kids?
Type: videocassette
Length: 90 min.
Date: 1994
Cost: $59.95
Source: PBS Video
Public Broadcasting Service
1320 Braddock Place
Alexandria, VA 22314-1698
(800) 344-3337

Poet Maya Angelou hosts a look at the Journey program, a small yet innovative program in Dallas, Texas, that attempts to reclaim the minds and hearts of inner-city gang members. The program follows a group of teenage boys to Journey's camp in east Texas, where they participate in an intensive three-day program of behavior modification.

Tip Line

WeTip
P.O. Box 1296
Rancho Cucamonga, CA 91729-1296
(909) 987-5005
(909) 987-2475 (FAX)
(800) 782-7463 (Tip Line)

A nationwide, crime-reporting anonymous tip line that provides 24-hour service, 365 days a year, to take information on all major crimes for the entire nation. The mission of this neutral, third-party citizens' group is to be the most effective anonymous citizens' crime-reporting resource in the nation. WeTip uses trained professional interviewers who know how to obtain information needed by investigators without compromising anonymity. Interviewers frequently work with law enforcement personnel and the anonymous citizen to obtain additional information. Citizen rewards are distributed on an anonymous basis, using case numbers and three-part code names.

WeTip will work with individual communities and school districts to develop programs tailored to community needs. Although WeTip began its program to combat drug trafficking, it has expanded to focus campaigns against such youth-related offenses as crimes against children, gang violence, graffiti, and juvenile firesetters. Holds an annual conference.

Glossary

Afrocentric curriculum   An educational violence prevention strategy that aims to prevent violence through an awareness of African and African-American roots and instill a sense of cultural identity and pride.

aggression reduction/anger management curriculum   An educational violence prevention strategy that conveys the message that anger is a normal human emotion and explores healthy and unhealthy ways to express and channel anger.

alternative setting   An alternative educational environment for dangerous and/or chronically disruptive students, either a separate room or a separate school.

Centers for Disease Control and Prevention   The leading U.S. federal agency for public health and injury control, which is now actively involved in violence prevention efforts and the evaluation of violence prevention programs.

character education   An educational strategy that attempts to teach and help clarify values, and help students become more caring individuals.

conflict resolution curriculum   An educational violence prevention strategy that helps develop empathy; impulse control; and skills in communication, problem solving, and anger management.

crime prevention/law-related education curriculum An educational violence prevention strategy that teaches students how to reduce their chances of becoming victims of crime and encourages them to develop school and community projects to reduce crime.

educational violence prevention strategies Curricula and instructional strategies that attempt to teach students behavior management skills, conflict resolution skills, and life skills.

environmental/technological violence prevention strategies Strategies designed to minimize hazards and risks in the environment by reducing exposure to violence and mitigating the results of it.

gang prevention/reduction curriculum An educational violence prevention strategy that builds awareness of the consequences of gang membership among youth who are not yet gang members.

Goals 2000: Educate America Act of 1994 Legislation that provides resources to states and communities to develop and implement education reforms that will help students reach academic and occupational standards.

Gun-Free Schools Act of 1994 (GFSA) Legislation mandating that every state receiving federal aid for elementary and secondary education must enact a law requiring school districts to expel from school for at least one year any student who brings a gun to school. Every state now has adopted such a law. Private schools are not subject to the provision of the GFSA. However, private school students who participate in local education agency (LEA) programs or activities are subject to the one-year expulsion requirement.

handgun violence prevention curriculum An educational violence prevention strategy that alerts students to the risk posed by handguns and helps them recognize and avoid potentially dangerous situations.

life skills training curriculum An educational strategy that teaches a range of social skills students need for healthy development, such as problem-solving skills, decision-making skills, and strategies for resisting peer pressure or media influences.

Metropolitan Life Survey of the American Teacher A survey conducted annually by Louis Harris and Associates that explores teachers' opinions and brings them to the attention of the U.S. public and policymakers.

National Education Goals Eight goals developed by U.S. governors in an attempt to create a framework of systematic education reform. They served as the basis for the Goals 2000: Educate America Act of 1994.

National School Safety Center A federal clearinghouse on school violence located in Westlake Village, California.

noradrenaline The "alarm hormone" that stimulates body chemicals and aids in the "fight or flight" response.

peace education curriculum   An educational violence prevention strategy that looks at violence prevention interpersonally and within and among societies as a whole.

peer mediation programs   Programs that train students and teachers to identify and mediate conflicts that occur in the school.

prejudice reduction/cultural awareness curriculum   An educational violence prevention strategy that attempts to overcome stereotypes and prejudices that foster violence.

regulatory strategies   Violence prevention strategies that impose academic, civil, and criminal penalties on certain unwanted behaviors to lower the risk of violence. They help establish school discipline policies and procedures that pertain to student behavior, creating alternative schools, and developing cooperative relationships with police and other government agencies.

role models curriculum   An educational violence prevention strategy that helps students learn lessons in nonviolent behavior by exploring the lives of exceptional historical or contemporary figures.

Safe and Drug-Free Schools and Communities Act of 1994 (SDFSCA)   Legislation that funds school violence prevention and substance abuse programs.

school uniforms   An environmental strategy thought to help decrease violence, theft, and gang activity, and to increase discipline and concentration on schoolwork.

self-esteem development curriculum   An educational violence prevention strategy that aims to raise students' self-esteem with the underlying assumption that doing so can improve academic performance and reduce violence.

serotonin   The "feel-good hormone" that keeps aggression in check. It has been intensively studied in human and animal research on violent behavior.

teen dating violence/family violence/sexual assault curriculum   An educational violence prevention strategy that addresses the increased incidents of domestic violence in recent years.

Telecommunications Bill of 1996   Legislation that deregulates the television industry, censors material deemed indecent on the Internet, and imposes prison fines and terms on those who make indecent material available over computer networks. An amendment to the bill requires television manufacturers to include a V-3 chip or comparable technology in every television set with a 13-inch or larger screen.

violence   A verbal, visual, or physical act intended to demean, harm, or infringe upon another's civil rights. Defined as a public health problem in the mid-1980s.

Violent Crime Control and Law Enforcement Act of 1995 Legislation that puts more police officers on the streets, funds new prison construction, imposes stiffer penalties on violent crimes, bans deadly assault weapons, and expands federal assistance for community-based crime prevention efforts.

Youth Risk Behavior Survey Conducted by the Youth Risk Behavior Surveillance System at the Centers for Disease Control and Prevention. Periodically measures the prevalence of priority health-risk behaviors among youth through national, state, and local surveys.

Index

For more than 20 years Deborah L. Kopka has specialized in the design, development, and delivery of educational media for youth and adults. She began her career as a teacher in a large urban high school and went on to serve as editorial director for a major educational publisher, where she collaborated with teachers and state departments of education to create middle school, high school, and postsecondary textbook programs. She currently works as an educational writer and journalist, as well as a consultant to major corporations on the development of training and educational programs.